Black Spot -
1 gal water
1. Tabsp. of bakeing soda
1 Tablespoon Vegetable oil
1 Tabsp - Fels - Naptha soap
solution

Gardening
for
Southern
Seasons

Super Seed Starter Tonic
2 gal water
1/4 cup of barnyard tea
1/4 cup soapy water

Monroe Garden Study League
Monroe, Louisiana

1/4 cup week tea

Member of The Garden Club of America

To share and encourage the love of gardening

Compiled and edited by:
Mrs. Kent Breard - Chairman
Mrs. J. McKenzie Sherrouse
Mrs. H. D. Touchstone
Mrs. Corbin Turpin
Mrs. Nelson Abell, III - Finance Chairman

With the editorial assistance of:
Mrs. Mona A. Oliver
  Assistant Professor of English
  Northeast Louisiana University
Mrs. R. L. Vanderpool, Jr.

Cynthia Day Neely - Cover design/Illustrator

ISBN: 0-9652405-0-9

First Printing 1988
Second Printing 1990
Third Printing 1996

Printed in the USA by

WIMMER
The Wimmer Companies, Inc.
Memphis

Acknowledgments

We are grateful to Dr. Edmund N. O'Rourke, Jr., Professor of Floriculture, Louisiana State University, and Dr. William A. Young, Louisiana State University Agricultural Center, for their inspiration and guidance.

We extend special thanks to Dr. John R. Pyzner and the Louisiana State University Cooperative Extension personnel for their services and valuable information.

We also thank the Louisiana Department of Natural Resources and the following interested people who contributed articles: Mr. Howard Gryder; Mrs. Woodrow Hathorn; Mr. Richard Johnson; Mr. Floyd Kent; Mr. B. Eugene King; Mrs. Robert McDowell, Jr.; Dr. Neil Odenwald; Joan A. Pitcher; Mr. D. Q. Rankin, Sr.; Mr. Robert Rickett; and Dr. R. Dale Thomas. We are indebted to the following club members who shared their gardening expertise: Mrs. Nelson Abell, Jr.; Mrs. Douglas Brown; Mrs. Grayson Guthrie; Mrs. A. Scott Hamilton; Mrs. Ivy Jordan; Mrs. C. J. Ledoux; Mrs. Jesse McDonald; Mrs. John Mullens; Mrs. A. B. Myatt, Jr.; Mrs. Amos Shelton; Mrs. George Trousdale; Mrs. Harold Woods, Sr.

Without the secretarial assistance of Mrs. Jan Ledoux and Mrs. Dawn Green this book would not have reached completion.

We gratefully acknowledge the generous grant from the Emy-Lou Biedenharn Foundation, without whose support this garden guide would not have been possible.

We extend special thanks to the following individuals and corporations for their encouragement and financial support: The Premier Bank, Mr. and Mrs. Nelson Abell, Mr. and Mrs. Nelson Abell, III, Mr. and Mrs. Ralph W. Brockman, Dr. and Mrs. Douglas C. Brown, Central Bank, Century Telephone Enterprises, Inc., First National Bank, Mr. and Mrs. William L. Husted, Dr. and Mrs. Ralph King, Jr., Louisiana Power and Light, Mr. and Mrs. C. J. Ledoux, Manville Forest Products Corporation, Mr. and Mrs. Jesse D. McDonald, Mrs. James W. Moore, Mr. and Mrs. John D. Mullens, Mr. and Mrs. James Norris, Security Bank, Mr. and Mrs. Amos Shelton, Mr. and Mrs. R. L. Vanderpool, Jr., Dr. and Mrs. James W. Wade, and Mrs. Harold Woods, Sr.

Special acknowledgment is also made to all the founding members of the Monroe Garden Study League who, through their combined efforts, have supported this publication.

Hortus III has been used as the source for botanical names.

A garden book for Zone 8 and surrounding areas.

The Monroe Garden Study League cordially invites you to visit the public gardens in our area:

ELSONG
The house and gardens   Monroe, Louisiana

BIBLE RESEARCH CENTER
   The Biblical garden   Monroe, Louisiana

BRIARWOOD - CAROLINE DORMAN
             NATURE PRESERVE   Saline, Louisiana

AMERICAN ROSE SOCIETY HEADQUARTERS   Shreveport, Louisiana

HODGES GARDEN   Many, Louisiana

KIROLI PARK   West Monroe, Louisiana

KALORAMA NATURE PRESERVE   Collinston, Louisiana

Preface

This is a gardening book prepared by amateurs*, in the sense of the word conveyed by the Latin origin of the term - lovers of gardening and all its diverse forms and activities. These amateurs have prepared their sections in the hope of sharing that love with others who already know the pleasures of gardening or with those who have yet to become enamored of this lifetime avocation. It quickly becomes apparent upon reading these sections that each of the authors demonstrates a different kind of participation in gardening and a different kind and level of expertise. All, however, demonstrate that love of gardening that makes them want to share their precious experiences with others. This is one of the aspects of gardening that makes it the number one avocation in the world.

The book begins with a look by each of four authors at a season in the gardening year, and again their writings show the various ways in which gardeners approach the subject and how they differ in their goals and enjoyment. This dealing with the seasons can also turn one's mind to the way gardening fits and adapts itself to the seasons of life - from childhood to the older years. The offer of reward is still there and the world of gardening is so diverse that all can share in it and enjoy it in their own fashion.

The book also demonstrates the social bonds that a shared love of gardening can forge. Nobody need be lonely where other gardeners are to be found, and where is that? <u>Everywhere</u>.

E. N. O'Rourke
Professor of Horticulture
Dept. of Horticulture
LSU, Baton Rouge, LA

*amateur *(L. <u>amator</u> lover)*. 1: one that has a marked fondness, liking, or taste. . . .

<u>Webster's Third New International Dictionary</u>

Contents

PLANTING AND PLANT CHARTS – cont'd.

GARDEN CARE

SOUTHERN FAVORITES

CARE OF CUT MATERIAL 149

MÉLANGE

GARDEN TERMS 190

INDEX 193

Special Note: Topsoil Tips indicated by green strip.

Introduction
to the Seasons

Planet Earth experiences seasonal changes because the axis of its daily rotation is tilted at approximately 23.5 degrees to the axis about which it makes its year-long orbit. As a result of this arrangement, the northern hemisphere of Earth has longer days and more concentrated energy from the sun's rays during the period between the third week in March and the third week in September than it does during the other half of the year. The longest day and the greatest energy concentration for the northern hemisphere happens in the middle of this period, on the day we call the first day of summer. On that day, the north pole of Earth is tilted closest to the sun, Monroe has 14 hours of daylight, and the sun doesn't set anywhere north of the Arctic Circle. The seasons are exactly reversed for the southern hemisphere, because the south pole must be slanted away from the sun at the same time the north pole is slanted toward the sun. In December, when Monroe has its first day of winter with only 10 hours of feeble daylight, while the beetles and blight spores slumber, while the gardener awaits the first spring seed catalog, the southern hemisphere is basking in summer comfort.

Bird, beast, and plant have learned to anticipate changes in the seasons. We don't really understand how they know when and how to prepare. They apparently sense the changing length of daylight, or temperature variations, or even star patterns. Ages ago, mankind learned to chart the seasons by erecting monuments like Stonehenge which point to the sun's rising or setting directions at special times of the year. Emerson once complained that modern man had lost his self-reliance by depending upon calendars and almanacs. But the ancient methods need not be totally lost. You could create your own Stonehenge by making a chart of your eastern or western horizon as seen from a convenient porch or window. Always stand in the same spot to make your observation and make notes of where the sun rises or sets all during the year. Mark the rising or setting points of the sun on your chart with seasonal jobs that need to be done. Then you can make your own gardening almanac with instructions like "Plant the turnips when the sun sets over the old cypress snag," or "Prune the roses when the sun rises next to the chimney on the Smith's house." May all your seasons be happy ones.

Robert M. Rickett
Associate Professor of Physics
Department of Physics
Northeast Louisiana University
Monroe, LA

Editor's Note:

When we think of the seasons, we think of winter, spring, summer, and fall. But when a teacher asked nine-year old Clay Oakley to name the seasons, his reply was "squirrel, quail, duck, and deer."

Winter

Flora on preceding page, shown clockwise:
  holly, camellia, forsythia, Japanese magnolia, pine,
  poinsettia, and pussy willow

Winter

December 21 - March 20

*He has made everything beautiful
in its time.*

Ecclesiastes 3:11a

The garden in winter can be as beautiful as in any other season. It need not be stark and bare. There are many lovely evergreens in varying shades with berries, seed pods, and flowers. At this season of the year, camellia and sasanqua bushes as well as pansies bloom to give color to the garden. Bring your garden into your home by cutting branches of evergreen shrubs with berries or flowers.

The winter solstice occurs around December 22 at which time the sun is farthest from the equator in the southern hemisphere; we have fewer hours of sunshine, and plants cease to grow and are dormant. Mother Nature slows down, seems to doze, and is sometimes covered with a blanket of snow. Now is the time for the gardener to reflect and enjoy his year's labor, even ease back in his arm chair and read seed catalogues.

Winter is a great time for making plans. First of all, decide what type of garden you want. It can range in size from a window box to many acres; let it be a reflection of you. Design it with the needs of your family in mind. Plan around outside activities they enjoy. If you feel inadequate, seek the help of a professional. Consider the maintenance - will you be the gardener or will it be someone you hire? To quote the publication <u>W</u>, "Puttering in your garden has style, leaving it all to the gardener doesn't." Keep it well groomed in all seasons. Strive for interest the year round using evergreens that have different shapes.

If your garden is already established, you may feel the need to make changes. Beds may be in the wrong places; they may be too small, too large, or need to be removed. Winter is the time to do this. As you make changes, keep in mind how much sun your beds get during the various seasons. This will determine the type of plant you use: one that requires full sun, partial sun, or shade. Use tall plants at the back of the bed; then graduate them to the ground. This gives a pleasing effect and helps the birds easily reach the ground for food and water. Select plants whose colors harmonize with the

exterior of your home. Mass planting is better than a variety of plants; too many varieties lose their effectiveness.

Trees are a very important part of the garden and can give you great pleasure. They form a background for your house and help insulate it. All else in your garden is governed by trees, so select them carefully, keeping in mind their shape, how fast they grow, and their life span. It is best not to plant too close to your house. The texture of the bark of some trees is very beautiful. They make lovely silhouettes as the sun shines through their branches, either bare in the winter or full of leaves in the summer.

Winter is also a good time to check garden tools; sharpen, repair, oil, or replace them. Put a light coat of oil over the metal parts. Drain your lawn mower for the season.

It's Time to Plan

Consider the needs of your family. Think of existing features you wish to emphasize: trees, specimen plants, or a fountain.

Outline and design your garden.

Chart a plan for a period of years.

Draw your plan to scale.

Select plants for shape, size, color, etc. Do you need regular size or dwarf? How fast does it grow? Will it need frequent pruning? Is the cost reasonable?

Order Caladium bulbs, perennial crowns, late spring and summer flowering bulbs, and seeds for spring planting.

Plan ahead for a night party or wedding by selecting annuals and vines that will give color for the evening. Pink, as well as white, is very beautiful at night. Moon Vine, Clematis, and Confederate Jasmine along with Petunias, Verbena, and Caladiums produce an effective look for evening.

It's Time to Plant

Trees

On Arbor Day trees are often planted as memorials.

Oak	Fruit *(pear, peach,*	Cypress
Magnolia	*apple, fig, mayhaw,*	Sassafras
Pine	*Japanese persim-*	Redbud
Dogwood	*mon, etc.)*	

14

Shrubs

Holly
Camellia
Azalea
Forsythia

Crape Myrtle
Ligustrum
Cherry Laurel
Wood Myrtle

Photinia
Cleyera

Bulbs

Crocus
Snow drop
Tulip - *last call to plant in January. Chill 6 weeks prior to planting.*

Hyacinth - *must be chilled before planting.*
Iris
Anemone

Gladiolus - *for constant bloom, plant every 2 weeks in February or March.*

Vines

Carolina Jasmine
Banksia Rose
Confederate Jasmine

Wisteria
Ivy
Fig Vine

Smilax

Ground covers

Monkey grass
Mondo
Thrift

Pachysandra
Liriope
Ajuga

Ivy
Charleston grass - *(Asian Jasmine)*

Roses

(See section on Roses)

Although winter is the coldest season, you can plant between cold snaps. In Zone 8, you can actually plant year round if you take the necessary precautions: protecting the roots, making a large hole for the plant so roots can spread, giving it plenty of water from the time it is planted until it is several years old. Burlap is good protection for roots when planting or transplanting. Use topsoil from the hole around the roots of your plant. Plant about one inch higher than desired; it will settle in time.

It's Time to Prune

Trees - best done in the winter

Crape Myrtles - Never prune severely. (Though it may make larger blooms, heavy pruning tends to destroy the unbroken lines of a smooth, tall trunk.)

Shrubs - only late summer and fall flowering shrubs (Do *NOT* prune spring flowering shrubs now.)

Azaleas - after they bloom

Camellias - after they bloom

Roses - around George Washington's birthday

Pansies - pinch old blooms for more buds.

January and February are the major pruning months. Many plants have beautiful seed pods, fruit, or foliage branches which, when pruned, can be brought into the house for beauty. Some cuttings, as you prune, can be rooted in peat moss, a sand mixture, or soil. Others can be rooted in a jar of water.

Prune for a desired shape; the natural form of a plant gives the best effect rather than a stiff, artificial look. Remove old wood by thinning out from the center of the shrub and cutting flush to the trunk. Delay pruning plants damaged by freeze until spring; you may be pleasantly surprised that they are still alive.

Do *NOT* cut bulb foliage.

It's Time to Water

Plants

Lawns

January and February are our coldest months. If the soil is dry, deep water to help plants and lawns withstand the cold. Do not water plants while frozen. Do not let water stand around the base of a plant. Seek drainage by lifting the plant or moving it. Yellow leaves may mean poor drainage. Mulch with oak leaves or pine straw, or cover with burlap, newspaper, or polyfilm to protect against the cold spell.

It's Time to Feed

Pansies

Iris

Sweet Peas

Shrubs

Camellias - feed again in six months. (See section on Camellias)

Azaleas - feed again in six weeks. (See section on Azaleas)

Trees - Drill a series of holes about 2" apart around the tree's "drip" line (where branches reach). Use a balanced fertilizer. Follow manufacturer's instructions.

Lawns - Your Extension Service (County Agent) will have your soil tested if you take a sample to the office to be advised as to your needs. Carefully follow instructions on fertilizer package; apply lime to lawn if needed.

It's Time to Force Branches to Bloom

Branches from spring flowering shrubs (e.g. forsythia, quince, pussy willow, and Japanese magnolia) may be cut and forced for early blooms in your home. Buds need to be forming on the branch before cutting. Split the ends of the branch and place it in warm water in a sunlit room. The length of time for the branch to show blooms depends on the maturity of the bud at the time you cut the branch; usually they appear within two weeks.

It's Time to Check for Insects and Diseases

Insects

> *Aphids*　　　　　　*Thrips*
> *Red Spiders*　　　*White Flies*
> *Scale*

Diseases

> *Canker* and *dieback* on Camellias
> *Brown patch* on lawns if winter is mild
> (Refer to sections on Insects and Diseases)

> Use a reputable person for spraying.

> *Late lies the wintry sun a-bed,*
> *A frosty, fiery, sleepy-head;*
> *Blinks but an hour or two;*
> *And then, a blood-red orange,*
> *Sets again.*
> 　　　　　. . .
> *Black are my steps on silver sod,*
> *Thick blows my frosty breath abroad;*
> *And tree and house, and hill, and lake,*
> *Are frosted like a wedding-cake.*
> 　　　　　　　*Robert Louis Stevenson*

Spring

Flora on preceding page, shown clockwise:
ivy, tulip, daisy, iris, daffodil, azalea

Spring
March 21 - June 20

*For, lo, the winter is past, the rain is over and gone; the flowers
appear on the earth, the time of the singing of birds is come,
and the voice of the turtle is heard in our land.*

Song of Solomon 2:11, 12

Swing into spring with pruning shears and weeders, with
seedlings and seeds. Spring is shape-up time in the garden.
Neatness, grooming, weeding, and pruning are all a part of the
beauty of spring. This is the season to enjoy the beauty of flowers
planted in the previous fall and winter and to plant for the bounty
of summer and fall. Remember spring brings daylight saving time
with longer evenings for gardening and enjoyment. From the
vernal equinox, when day and night are equal, to the summer
solstice, when the day is the longest, the beauty, joy, and glory of
the garden reflect the time and effort of the gardener.

As nature comes to life in the spring, it is easier to spot
necessary changes. Ride around the neighborhood or take a boat
ride along the bayous (waterways). Observe other gardens, develop a "seeing eye" with careful attention to detail, write down
ideas to remember, sketch or photograph anything of special
interest. Be inspired by what others are doing. The nicest compli-
ment is to adapt others' ideas to your own needs. Remember a
well-landscaped home, church, school, or park will increase the
value of everyone's property. Enjoy the beauty of spring in all its
glory.

It's Time to Plan

Evaluate, re-think, and write down priorities for the landscape.

Decide between the many choices for you and your family's
lifestyle.

> An entertainment area for cook-outs, play yards, a pool, lawn
> games, and the fun of outdoor living
>
> A quiet area for relaxation, reading, and visiting with friends
>
> A more formal garden with walks, pruned hedges, and
> stylized plants
>
> A garden with simplicity of design (often the most elegant)

Fencing or the use of evergreen shrubs to soften noises, give privacy, and provide security

Masses of color

A naturalized area

Low maintenance

Consider

Energy conservation (e.g. trees for protection against summer sun or as windbreaks)

Drainage (e.g. water standing in ditches)

It's Time to Plant

Annuals and Perennials

Ageratum	Marigold	Portulaca
Alyssum	Moonflower	Salvia
Coleus	Geranium	Sunflower (seeds
Cosmos	Periwinkle	for birds)

Bulbs

Caladium	Lycoris	Water lily
Canna	Dahlia	Hosta
Liriope	Gladiolus	Tuberose
Daylily	Calla	Butterfly lily
Violets		

Remove, dig, divide, and share or transplant bulbs after foliage dies. Plant in groups or drifts for the most effect in the landscape.

Shrubs

Hydrangea	Abelia	Oleander
Gardenia	Rose	Lantana
Crape Myrtle	Althea	Azalea

Preparation is the number one priority. Before planting, check to see if soil is friable. After spring rains, rub soil between fingers to see if it is dry enough to work. If soil is too wet or dry, a handful of dirt squeezed will not stay in a ball. Dig a big hole for a small plant ($5 hole for a $1 plant).

Over planting is a great temptation for the novice and professional. In our climate it can only result in crowding, extra pruning, and more transplanting.

It's Time to Prune

Prune winter damaged shrubs after new growth reveals dead or injured branches. Prune again immediately after blooming. Remember cuttings can be enjoyed in the house.

Shape hydrangeas. (See section on Hydrangeas)

Prune hedges, espaliered plants, and topiary forms to keep from losing shape as they grow rapidly now.

Narrow boxwood hedges at the top to allow sun to reach bottom branches.

Disbud or pinch out top bud of annuals and perennials to encourage bloom and bushiness.

"Deadhead" bulbs (snip faded bloom), but do not remove foliage until it dies.

Remove dead and damaged leaves from ferns and aspidistra.

Remove caladium flower stalks. They weaken the plant.

Most plants are pruned according to their natural growth. (See section on Pruning)

It's Time to Water

When planting or transplanting

During a rare dry spring, using a soaker hose about one hour once a week. Water in the morning rather than evening to avoid mildew, black spot, etc. Watering during midday will scorch plants.

A rain gauge is fun and lets you know the amount of rainfall in your garden.

Be careful never to step in beds saturated from rain or watering; it compacts the soil.

It's Time to Feed

New Perennials - 8-8-8 lightly or manure

Bulbs - after they finish blooming

Roses - 8-8-8 monthly. (See section on Roses)

Established shrubs and plants - 8-8-8. Spring flowering shrubs after they bloom

Hollies and *Maidenhair fern* - light feeding of Epsom salts after blooming. (A tried and true, cheap, and readily available source of magnesium.) Use 1 tablespoon per gallon of water.

Hydrangeas - to change color: aluminum sulfate for blue, lime for pink

Evergreens, deciduous trees and *shrubs, ground covers,* and *perennials* lightly a second time before summer

Houseplants, begonias, and *geraniums* as you water, with a weekly weak solution of soluble fertilizer. Many good brands are available.

Remember to check soil pH before selecting the kind of fertilizer needed.

It's Time To Groom

Edge walks, driveway, and patios.

Weed flower beds, around trees and specimen shrubs before using mulch.

Mulch using peat moss, pine straw, leaves, plastic mulch, newspaper, bark, or gravel.

Stake tall, limber plants.

Never mulch with pecan or magnolia leaves. Pecan leaves harbor diseases and magnolia leaves do not break down easily.

As you groom, check for signs of diseases and insects. (See sections on Insects and Diseases) Early spring is the time to treat shrubs with a dormant oil spray to prevent scale.

It's Time to Cut and Share Blooms and Plants

Branches of azaleas, dogwoods, and spirea

Bulbs that are crowded, such as native iris, daffodils

Ground covers that have spread too rapidly

Seedlings growing beneath mature trees, camellias, holly, and other shrubs

Climbing plants, such as clematis, jasmine, Lady Banksia that need to be kept under control

Roses, to increase blooms

Bouquets for Easter baskets, May Day or graduation, Mother's Day, Father's Day, and spring weddings

The hazards of spring are high winds, too much rain, and early or late frosts. To protect young plants from frost, cover them with newspaper, plastic blankets, or place a discarded milk or juice carton over each. Covering must be removed in the warmth of the day.

And the spring arose in the garden fair
And the spirit of Love fell everywhere;
And each flower and herb on Earth's dark breast
Rose from the dreams of its wintry rest.

Percy Bysshe Shelley

Summer

Flora on preceding page, shown clockwise:
hibiscus, rose, caladium, zinnia, fern, and petunia

Summer
June 21 - September 20

. . . Whatsoever things are lovely . . . think on these things.

Philippians 4:8

In the good ole summer time

'Tis the season for armloads of flowers, rich harvest, and baskets brimming with garden grown vegetables; a time for vacations, cool lemonade, relaxed living; a time to "smell the daisies" in one's secret garden away from the busy world – and a time for mowing, raking, watering.

Summer annuals and summer perennials show off their color trying to "outdo" one another. If one is tired of color, then it's time for sitting in the shade of the old oak tree surrounded by a cool green and white garden. Most of the garden work is done but there are still chores to keep the back limber, the mind sharp, and the spirit free. Summer is as Webster says, "a season of the finest development, perfection, or beauty."

It's Time to Plan

Review your plan drawn in the winter months. Having planned your garden successfully by using plants best suited to the location in size for less pruning, color for your lifestyle, disease resistance, and water needs, you'll find your summer maintenance is minimal. Gardening is a creative joy, however, and a good gardener never stops reviewing and improving.

Decide what is needed to improve the landscape: adding a tree, more flowering shrubs; removing something; or perhaps creating a garden retreat. Daydreams are better in a secret garden.

Consider locations for shrubs to have continuous summer blooms next year.

Early summer	*Mid-summer*	*All summer*
Hydrangea	Althea	Roses
Abelia	Gardenia	

Check the garden for shade.
Is there too much?

What limbs should be cut for light to grow grass?

Where is shade needed to reduce the heat of summer? Decide where to plant a tree for shade by taking a pole, placing it in the ground, and watching for the summer shadows.

Order daffodils in early summer.

Order tulips in late summer.

It's Time to Plant

For a bright, showy flower bed:

Annuals and Perennials

Impatiens	Portulaca	Sedum
Ageratum	Petunia	Cosmos
Marigold	Begonia	Balsam
Geranium	Four O'Clock	Sage
Hibiscus	Gloriosa	
Gerbera Daisy	Vinca	

Bulbs

Water lily	Amaryllis	Iris
Watsonia	Lycoris Radiata	Zephyranthes *(rain*
Colchicum	Lycoris Squamigera	*lily)*
Gladiolus corm	Violet	
Day lily	Crinum	

For a soothing, cool green and white garden:

Snow on the	White Impatiens	Caladium
Mountain	Fern	Fatsia
White Vinca	Begonia	Aspidistra

For fall color:

Chrysanthemum	Ageratum	Geranium
Ornamental	Cockscomb	Colchicum
Pepper	Marigold	
Copper Plant	Sternbergia	
Jacobs Coat	Hibiscus	

For a green lawn in winter:

Rye grass - sow seeds in late summer

It's Time to Prune

Annuals and perennials - remove and burn diseased or dead foliage from plants.

Crysanthemums - pinch back regularly until mid-July to have full, bushy plants.

Caladiums - remove flower stalks to encourage new leaf growth.

Bearded Iris - cut foliage in a fan shape when it begins to turn brown at the tips. This will give stronger, larger flowers.

Roses

Hybrid Teas & Floribundas - prune lightly in mid-summer for fall blooms and stronger stems. Keep blossoms cut off of blooming plants for healthy, abundant leaves and blossoms. Cut to just above an outside leaf with five (5) leaflets.

Climbing roses - thin when needed after blooming. Remove dead and diseased canes.

Hydrangeas *(See Hydrangeas)*

Gardenias - remove dead wood and old blooms.

Hedges - trim in late September for the last time before winter.

Wisteria - prune green runners by one half and root-prune to keep the vine controlled.

Crape Myrtles - cut the blossoms off after they finish the first bloom for a second bloom. Prune in late summer after the flowers have completed their blooming cycle so the tree silhouette can be enjoyed. Remember, their trunks are as beautiful as the blossoms – a natural sculpture.

Plants or trees to be moved in the fall - root-prune in late summer, cutting with a sharp spade. Don't cut all around at once; cut two sides not too close to the trunk. Wait several weeks and cut the other two (2) sides. (See sections on Trees and Pruning)

Lawns - mow regularly to prevent seed heads from forming. Don't mow too closely in the heat of summer. Raise mower blades as high as possible. The dry, hot days will burn the roots and kill the grass. Avoid bumping or nicking trunks of young trees and shrubs since these cuts can severely damage, even kill your plant.

Start a compost pile with grass clippings and leaves. Add fertilizer occasionally and turn the pile often, keeping it moist.

Remember: "Any weed that goes to seed — Next year you'll regret the deed."

It's Time to Water

New plants - for a healthy start

Second year plants - to keep them growing

Azaleas and camellias - in late summer for spring blooms

Lawns

The most important summer need is water. Most plants need soaking until the water penetrates the soil several inches. Shrubs need at least 12" of water; trees need even more. Let the water dribble on the plant or bed for at least 30 minutes; then check the depth of water penetration. Deep soaking once a week during a dry spell develops good, strong, deep roots. Too little water causes roots to reach up for water, doing more harm than good. Occasionally, a light misting on the leaves cools the plant without bruising the blossoms.

Watering at the right time is very important. Preferably, one should water in the early morning whenever the soil is noticeably dry or when the plants show early signs of distress such as little new growth, dull or grey-green leaves, browning at the tip or edge of leaves. Noonday wilting does not indicate a need for water. Never water in the noonday sun for fear of scalding your plants. Afternoon is permissible if the plant has time to dry before night; otherwise bugs will have a feast.

It's Time to Feed

Chrysanthemums - every two weeks with a light application of fertilizer.

Pot plants and blooming plants - frequent light feedings rather than one heavy feeding

Lawns - light feeding in mid to late summer

Thunderstorms come during the growing season just when they are needed. Lightning - even without the rain - brings nitrogen to earth.

Late feeding of shrubs will cause new growth that can be injured by an early freeze.

It's Time to Reap the Benefits of Your Garden

Cut Flowers:

Ageratum	Coreopsis	Marigold
Begonia	Crape Myrtle	Roses
Clematis	Geranium	Salvia
Green Hydrangea	Hibiscus	Canna
Blanket Flower	Dahlia	Verbena
Butterfly Bush	Day Lily	Zinnia
Butterfly Weed	Goldenrod	Daisy
Blackberry Lily	Tuberose	
Rain Lily	Lycoris	

Cut Cool, Green Foliage:

Aspidistra	Euonymus	Pine
Caladiums	Elaeagnus	Hosta
Fatsia	Yew	Pittosporum
Magnolia	Coleus	Aucuba
Banksia Rose	Ferns	

Extend your harvest by preserving material for winter arrangements and gifts.

Dry Flowers & Foliage:

By Hanging

Buckeye	Mimosa pods	Celosia
Dock	Nandina	Seed Pods
Magnolia cone	Hydrangea	Herbs
Catalpa	Cattails	Goldenrod

In Silica Gel or Borax & Sand

Blackeyed Susan	Marigold	Thistle
Calendula	Lantana	Zinnia
Carnation	Daisy	Roses
Chrysanthemum	Sunflower	

In Glycerin

Dogwood	Pittosporum	Ivy
Elaeagnus	Mahonia	Loquat
Eucalyptus	Photinia	Magnolia
Forsythia	Oak	

General rules for drying plant material:

Cut flowers just before they reach maturity (some in bud stage, half-open stage, and almost full bloom); strip leaves.

For glycerin method, do not condition first. Use 1/2 glycerin, 1/2 hot water up to 2" on stems. Cut foliage in its growing period. Water is absorbed faster then.

If using a drying compound or hanging, place material in a dark, dry area after conditioning. Do not leave in the drying compound too long.

In our hot, dry summer, many flowers can be dried by placing them in a box or bag and then in the car trunk. In a week or less they will be dried.

Press Flowers & Foliage:

Ferns - place fronds on waxed paper or white tissue paper. Cover with another sheet of the waxed paper or tissue paper and several layers of newspaper. Weight with a heavy book or place under a heavy rug for several weeks.

This procedure can be used on other flowers such as pansies, violets, larkspur, geranium leaves, and fall leaves.

As summer ends
Propagate:

Aucuba	Abelia	Holly
Pittosporum	Viburnum	Azaleas
Yellow Jasmine	Hydrangeas	Gardenias
Crape Myrtle	Camellias	Boxwood
Ivy *(in late summer)*	Ligustrum	Butterfly Bush
	Sasanquas	

Pot:

New plants to bring in for the winter

Impatiens - for the house so you can enjoy the bloom inside all winter. New plants can be rooted to put out in the garden next summer.

Groom houseplants that need to be brought inside:

Check for insects or strange larvae so that you won't be surprised if a night moth hatches in the bedroom or a tiny snake appears for tea!

Revive neglected houseplants by loosening the soil and applying fresh soil on top. Water afterwards.

Place a pot of basil in the kitchen for winter use.

Mulch beds at least 2" deep for winter protecton and to keep the weeds down.

Send the children to school.

Start to sing

> *Tell me, sunny goldenrod growing everywhere,*
> *Did fairies come from fairyland and weave the dress*
> *you wear?*

Fall

Flora on preceding page, shown clockwise:
spider lily, tallow, chrysanthemum, pyracantha, oak leaf,
and yarrow

Fall

September 21 - December 20

*As long as the earth remains, there will be
springtime and harvest, cold and heat, winter
and summer, day and night.*

Genesis 8:22

The warmth of late autumn days tend to lull one into the tranquil feeling of Indian summer - a period for enjoying the final flourish of the garden's bloom, watching the lush greens of summer change to burnished gold, and anticipating the unfolding of another season.

The cooling winds hurl the leaves down into a canopy of colors - red, yellow, orange, and brown. Although not as dramatic as a New England landscape in the fall, the beauty of the various maples, Chinese tallows, dogwoods, cypresses, ginkgoes, sassafrases, and other trees afford lovely settings in the Southern garden.

Now is a wonderful time to buy trees that are showing their seasonal color. According to folklore, when one buys a sassafras tree, one is buying a bit of Southern history. The dried leaves from this tree are ground and used in Cajun cuisine for thickening gumbo. Also, the fresh roots can be boiled in water to produce a refreshing tea.

The days of maturity from the September equinox to the December solstice are ones of constant change in the garden and require planning, preparation, and work for the gardener.

Fall is a perfect time to plant and transplant trees and shrubs. The warm soil produces new roots; thus, the plants become established before cooler weather and can take advantage of winter rains.

Additional beds can be prepared now if needed, or perhaps the existing ones need to be widened. Rose beds can be dug now and selections made for later planting.

This is also "clean-up" time for the gardener. Clear away all dead annuals and clean the flower beds. Rake leaves and add those that are suitable to the compost pile. Good grooming does a lot for a garden that is "out-of-bloom."

All garden hardware and equipment lasts longer if given the proper care. Drain your garden hoses that you won't need and store them with sprinklers for use in the spring. Also, clean gutters as the overflow from rains can damage plants.

Feed the birds! Feed the fish in the lily pond!

Fall includes some of the most joyous holidays. Consider giving plants and/or tools as gifts. Prepare for Thanksgiving, Christmas, and Hanukkah! This is a joyous season. "Perhaps Mother Nature did save the best for last."

It's Time to Plan
Reflect

Is your winter landscape working?

What needs to be changed? Added?

Have you overplanted, resulting in overwork for yourself or your gardener?

Study the framework of your garden as the plants begin to go dormant.

Are your shrubs and trees placed where they give the garden structure and focus?

Order bulbs if you haven't done so. When selecting your bulbs, remember that there are early, mid-season, and late blooming varieties.

Think about starting or adding to a compost pile (See Planting section)

It's Time to Plant
Trees

Oak	Magnolia	Cherry
Mimosa	Ginkgo	Chinese Tallow
Crape Myrtle	Elm	Japanese Maple
Loquat	Birch	Willow
Crabapple	Dogwood	Pear
Plum	Peach	Redbud
Fringe Tree	Cypress	Sassafras

Shrubs

Camellia	Nandina	Pyracantha
Sasanqua	Gardenia	Pussy Willow
Elaeagnus	Photinia	Abelia
Aucuba	Forsythia	Viburnum
Rhododendron	Deutzia	Quince
Boxwood	Holly	
Azalea	Euonymus	

In planting trees and shrubs, group several of the same variety for harmony in the landscape design.

Grasses

"hot weather"
St. Augustine
Zoysia
Centipede
Bermuda

"winter grass"
Rye grass - Sow in late September, half the seed from one direction, the remainder from the opposite direction.

Annuals and Perennials

Bedding Plants:

Pansies	Calendula	Dianthus
Peonies	Sweet Williams	Stock
Chrysanthemums	Snapdragons	Verbena
Phlox	Shasta Daisies	Ornamental grasses

Seeds to Sow:

Larkspur	Pinks	Cornflower
Early Sweet Pea	Alyssum	Wildflowers
Candytuft	Nasturtium	California Poppy

Bulbs

October:

Daffodils	Narcissus

November:

Snowdrops	Paper White	Grape Hyacinth
Easter Lily	Narcissus - in	Calla Lily
Ginger Lily	rocks & water	Dutch Iris
Ranunculus	around Thanks-	Oxalis
("feet" down)	giving to bring	Crocus
Anemone ("eye"	indoors for the	
up)	holidays	

December-January

Tulips and Hyacinths - refrigerate 4-6 weeks; then plant bulbs with pointed ends up. Water thoroughly.

Bulbs planted in shady areas or on the north side of the house will bloom later and last longer. A reliable bulb retailer can provide help.

Obviously, if it is time to plant them, it is also time to divide perennials and transplant or share them. Divide hosta before the leaves die. Also dig and divide gladiolus corms, irises, daylilies, dahlias.

Caladiums can be dug, dried, and stored in stockings or peat moss in a dry, warm place for planting the following spring.

Mark the location of newly planted bulbs and perennials.

Ground covers

Ajuga	Liriope
Pachysandra	English Ivy

Don't forget: Ivy is known to sleep, then creep, then leap! Allow for growth.

Vines

Muscadine	Clematis	Wisteria

Herbs

Chives	Dill	Winter Savory
Garlic	Sage	

Roses *(See section on Roses)*

When you are planting, your soil type, plant quality, and growth habits are all significant factors. Conditions are more important than a time table; growth response is good if the soil is right. Soil must be easily pulverized when dug about 6 inches. Small plants grow quicker and are easier to transplant. The root system is more important than the size of the plant. Don't sacrifice quality for quantity.

During planting time, transplant mistakes. Don't nurse a sick plant; replace it.

Now is also a good time to re-pot houseplants if necessary before bringing inside. Allow three weeks before heat is turned on in the house.

It's Time to Prune

Annuals and perennials - pinch back to encourage last bloom

Shrubs and trees - all if needed, except spring flowering shrubs
   Oak leaf hydrangeas - only variety to be pruned now

Roots - all shrubs to be transplanted
   Wisteria - 30" -40" from trunk if plant did not bloom

Pruning is done to shape, control, and encourage new growth because plants will thicken where cut. Use sharp tools, cut on a slant, but don't butcher the plant.

It's Time to Water

Trees and *shrubs* - newly planted and transplanted

Camellias and *azaleas* to keep moist. Water foliage frequently.

Bulb beds that have been newly planted

Seeds that have been sown

Houseplants - keep moist but do not saturate.

Water the garden well before the last mulch is applied, and water deeply before a freeze is expected. This insures plants a better chance to survive the cold.

It's Time to Feed

Annuals - lightly with water soluble fertilizer (e.g. 5-10-10)

Chrysanthemums - every 3 weeks, until buds show color (e.g. 8-8-8)

Bulbs - that have been planted for several years

Camellias - with a special Azalea-Camellia fertilizer when they finish blooming

Nandinas and Hollies - with a high phosphate fertilizer (e.g. 0-14-14). They will hold berries longer.

Roses - established bushes (See section on Roses).

Transplants - with any complete fertilizer (e.g. 8-8-8)

Rye Grass - with a complete fertilizer one month after planting

Pot plants - before bringing into the house

Compost pile - with fertilizer high in nitrogen. And keep turning over and watering.

It's Time to Groom

Mulch

    Bulb beds - with dry leaves. Remove at end of winter.

    Shrubs and *perennials* - newly planted or transplanted

    Azaleas

    Camellias

    Maidenhair ferns

Mulching protects plants from the cold. An early frost is a possibility.

Stake - all tall plants (e.g. Chrysanthemums) to protect against wind and heavy rains.

As you are grooming, watch for brown patch on lawns, aphids and cutworms, and for the first predicted freeze.

Spray houseplants and roses for insects, camellias for scale.

Treat camellias with gibberellic acid for larger blooms. (See section on Camellias)

It's Time to Harvest

Pods and berries

French Mulberry - purple

Smilax - green to black

Pyracantha - gold to orange to red

Hollies - green, yellow, red

Nandina berries - pink to orange to red. Cut just as they show pink; allow to dry naturally for fall dried arrangements

Cattails - spray with hair spray or lacquer type spray to preserve

Tallow berries - cut as they begin to open

Magnolia pods

Flowers

Chrysanthemums - dazzling colors of bronze, yellow, orange, white, magenta, pink, and shades of red

Roses - heavenly colors, heavenly fragrance

Gerbera Daisies - yellow, orange, red, white, gold, magenta

Stokesia - white, blue (closes at night)

Hydrangea - green, pink, blue, purple, brown, or beige (will often dry on the bush)

Butterfly lilies - White and fragrant

Spider lilies - red, pink, yellow

Zinnias, Marigolds - multicolored, can be dried

Goldenrod -it's lovely used in arrangements and is sneeze proof (says the A.M.A.!) It will also dry.

Pine cones - for a colorful blaze in the fireplace, treat pine cones with the following solution:

    2 gallons water   1 1/2 lbs. rock salt

    1 lb. copper sulphate

Use a large bucket and mix this solution well before adding cones. Submerge the cones for three weeks. Dry thoroughly.

Gather pumpkins and grapevines as well as pine cones and seed pods for decorations.

Make "grapevine" wreaths and other decorations.

Soak holiday greens in water for about 12-24 hours. Store in a cool place and keep moist. They will last for weeks.

Force branches of flowering shrubs (e.g. quince, forsythia) if the weather has been moderate and buds have formed.

> *Come, little leaves, said the wind one day*
> *Come o'er the meadow with me and play;*
> *Put on your dresses of red and gold,*
> *For summer is gone and the days grow cold.*
>
>   *George Cooper*

Planting
&
Plant Charts

Planting Basics

Before planting can begin, you must first make a decision. What kind of garden do you want? Would you prefer one that requires lots of intensive care or one that can take care of itself at times that you want to make a trip? Do you want to grow just ornamental plants or fruits or vegetables as well? If you don't have a yard or have only a small outdoor area, do you want an indoor garden or a container garden? A beginner can always change as interests change, develop, or lessen. A good plan for the more permanent garden features takes into account the changing nature of plans and plants. Beginners should try things that have a high chance of success, then move on to more challenging projects. Some plants are the basis for social activities, such as the Rose Society, Camellia Society, etc., and if this aspect is desirable, a beginner could start with these plants and learn from other club members about their experiences.

Next, read about it. Once a decision is made about the kind of gardening activity a beginner wants to try, there is a variety of sources to consult for information. You may find that you are not as interested in gardening as you thought, or you may be encouraged even more after doing a little reading. Be observant! Look at what other gardeners are doing in your area, and if you think you would like to try something similar, at least you have an idea that this will work in your area. (Some of the gardening ideas you read about from other areas will not work here.) The selection of plant material in an area is usually based on long-term adaptability. Exotics may grow for a while but will usually be disappointing in the long run - except for those people who relish the challenge of growing, or trying to grow, exotic materials.

Established garden center operators should be prepared and happy to offer tips. Be wary of the advice of people who have not been in the business long, or of the temporary help in garden centers or stores. They may not know any more than you do, but will be eager to appear knowledgable.

Starting

How do I start once I have decided on the kind of gardening I want? This will depend largely on the type of gardening. Indoor gardening and container gardening are special topics that come in later. Outdoor gardening involves many of the same things, but in some cases we are stuck with features of soil, site, topography, neighboring buildings

and trees, etc. and must work with what is there. So, let's look at some considerations of outdoor gardening.

Site

The area available will limit some choices. Available light is an important feature. Many plants need 6 to 8 hours of direct sunlight to prosper. Others can stand shade; some require shade. Lawns don't grow well under trees, and tree roots, especially on heavy soils, compete strongly for water and nutrients. Gardening under trees is possible, but calls for special attention.

A new site with no trees allows decisions to be made about the types and the placement of trees. They may be evergreen or deciduous; small, medium, or large; long-lived or short-lived. (The County Agent has a good bulletin on trees, as an example of sources of information available.) All trees drop leaves at times, but some, like magnolias, have durable leaves that cause some special problems. A site with existing trees calls for plans that work with all or some of the trees. Some trees may be so poorly sited that it is better to remove them, or they may be in bad condition. Remember that trees, like all plants, grow larger as long as they remain alive. So in your plans try to visualize the tree's impact on other plants some years ahead. This holds true for shrub planting as well.

Landscapes are not static. Plants change in size and shape as they age, and they don't live forever. A sunny area may become shaded in a few years. Good advice on landscaping is available through the County Agent's office.

Soils

Soils for outdoor gardens need to be evaluated. Help in taking a soil sample and in interpreting the test results is again available from the County Agent's. It may be that the soil will need amendments for the plants you want to grow. If so, the County Agent can make recommendations.

In the beginning know your soil.

Clays - small particles. High nutrient. Water retention capacity. Holds sand and silts together for better soil structure. Difficult to work.

Sands - Coarsest of soil particles. Drains rapidly, washing away nutrients and sand with it.

Loam - good balance of sand, clay, and humus. Most fertile of all. Easiest to work. Ideal - generally the darker the loam, the better.

Topsoil depth affects the plant growth. Trees and shrubs need about 2'-4'; annuals, 1'-2'; Perennials, 1' to 2'.

Drainage

Proper drainage can not be stressed enough. Without it there will be no successful gardening. The natural slope of the garden should drain easily. If this is not the case, a professional or your County Agent can suggest ways for you to correct this condition by using a drainage system or regrading the plot. However, simply planting on a slope does not always mean the drainage is good. It depends upon the soil.

Ideally, your soil should consist of small particles of earth, humus, airspace, and water. Sandy soil drains too quickly, carrying the valuable nutrients with it. Clay soil holds the water too long and can cause the plants to be waterlogged. In both cases the natural support of the root system of the plants has been weakened by the drainage.

A strong root system is needed to carry water and oxygen through the plant. As the water runs off, it draws air and nutrients into the soil for the plant's use.

One way to check your drainage is to dig a deep hole and fill it with water. The water should be absorbed in 10-15 minutes. If it takes an hour, check the quality of your soil. If the texture and quality of the soil is not the problem, dig deeper to see if there is a layer of hardpan (clay) soil that is so compacted that water and plant roots can not penetrate it.

In some cases raised flower beds can be the solution to this problem. Consult a professional when necessary.

Preparation of Beds

Outline the area with string, cornmeal, flour, or a hose

Remove the sod and any weeds

Work the soil prior to planting. Add compost, leaf mold, peat moss, or sand to insure proper drainage, water holding abilities, and aeration of the soil. If drainage is poor, raise the bed. Smooth the area with a rake.

Compost

A compost pile is an asset for a gardener if there is space for it. Into this, table scraps, leaves, newspaper, wood chips, bark, etc. are added. Do not add magnolia or pecan leaves to the compost pile. Fertilizer is applied often. The pile should be turned at least once a

week. More detailed instructions can be found in your garden books or your public library.

If you do not have a compost pile, consider having an area to pile leaves and grass clippings. To this pile add fertilizer and water occasionally. If you can, turn it. Fall leaves should be dried by mid-spring and ready for the flower beds. This organic matter is most important for a good garden.

Learn more about organic gardening. Even on a small scale, re-cycling helps conservation. You can do your part to make the world a little better.

Tools To Aid Planting

The material used and the type of construction determine the quality of tools. Quality tools are worth the additional cost since they usually feel better in the hand, last longer, and are easier to use. They save time and labor. Try different types and sizes of tools to find those best suited to the user. Women generally prefer shorter and lighter weight tools.

Care and use determine the life of the tool. Clean and oil the blades to prevent rust. Linseed oil protects wooden handles. Rust can be removed with steel wool.

<u>Cultivating</u>
Hoes
Rakes
Spades & Spading fork
Shovels
Trowels
Hand cultivators

<u>Cutting</u>
Shears–for flowers
   Anvil blade – for pruning
Loppers
Hedge clippers
Pruning saws

<u>Watering</u>
Hoses
Sprinklers
Watering cans
Soakers
Nozzles for spraying, misting,
  heavy streams

<u>Mechanical</u>
Mowers
Weeders
Edgers
Hedge clippers

The single most important tool for the home gardener is a flat-bladed file with a wooden handle to sharpen tools.

WHAT TO PLANT	WHEN TO PLANT	HOW TO PLANT

GRASS

St. Augustine
Zoysia
Centipede
Bermuda *(will invade flower bed)*

Anytime but better in
   spring or fall

Seed
Sod
Sprig

Rye Grass   Late summer   Seed

TREES

See section on Trees

November through March
November through March
Anytime – (keep damp)

Barerooted
Balled
Containers

SHRUBS

See section on Shrubs

November through March
November through March
Anytime – (keep damp)
Fall or spring

Barerooted
Balled
Containers
Seeds

ANNUALS & PERENNIALS

Depends upon variety and
time of bloom

Barerooted
Containers
Cuttings
Layering
Seeds

WHAT TO TRANSPLANT

Shrubs
Trees
Perennials

WHEN TO TRANSPLANT

All seasons if care is given.
Fall and spring preferred.

HOW TO TRANSPLANT

1. Dig hole (twice the size of ball) before lifting plant.
2. Mark front of plant.
3. Take as many roots as possible.
4. Set plant at same depth as before.
5. Fill in with good soil; pack it as you go.
6. Water and mulch.
7. Cut back 1/3 - 2/3.
8. Check with Extension Service about the use of rooting agents.

Annuals

An annual is a plant that completes its life cycle in one year. Its seed is planted; it grows, flowers, sets seeds, and dies. Its purpose is to reproduce plants. This being true, it stands to reason that if the plant does not set seed, it will continue to grow and produce flowers. With the right conditions, annuals will bloom longer if the flowers are kept cut.

When planning your garden, use annuals for color outside just as you use color in your home.

Annuals can be planted by seeds, or purchased as small bedding plants at the garden shops.

Know the color, size, and growing conditions before purchasing them. Most annuals require good soil and good light. Many of the newer varieties are disease resistant and have much larger flowers than were available in the past. Read carefully the cultural instructions before planting.

Preferably, select nursery plants not yet in bloom.

Fertilize the seeds two weeks after they are sown, then every 4 -6 weeks throughout the growing season. Use a high phosphorus fertilizer (e.g. 10-20-10).

On annuals that have colorful foliage like the copper plant, caladium, and coleus, use a complete fertilizer (e.g. 8-8-8) since prolonged use of a high nitrogen fertilizer will cause excessive greening.

One of the simplest ways to fertilize is to use a soluble fertilizer that can be applied as you water your plants.

ANNUALS

COMMON NAME	PLANTING TIME	HEIGHT	COLOR	REMARKS
Ageratum Floss Flower *Ageratum houstonianum*	March-June	6-24"	White, blue, rose	Propagated by cuttings. Not always true from seed.
Alyssum-Sweet Madwort *Lobularia maritime*	January-March September-November	3-6"	White, violet	Long blooming season. Rock gardens.
Baby's Breath *Gypsophila elegans*	September-March	20-24"	White	Free-growing plant. Reseeds. Plants bloom out quickly.
Balsam Garden Type *Impatiens balsamina*	March-September	15-24"	Pink, rose, white	Full sun. Rich soil. Good container plant.
Begonia *Semperflorens*	April-September	6-9"	Pink, white, red	Partial shade. Rich moist soil. Good for indoors.
Calendula Pot Marigold *Calendula officinalis*	September-November	12-15"	Yellow, orange	Resists light frost. Attacked by aphids.
Candytuft *Iberis umbellata*	September-March	10-15"	White, red, lavender	Rock gardens. Hardy. Dwarf-growing.
Chinese Forget-Me-Not *Cynoglossum Amabile*	September-March	20-30"	Blue, pink	Withstands hot, dry conditions.
Clarkia "	March-April	1-3'	White, pink	Hardy. Long blooming season.

COMMON NAME	PLANTING TIME	HEIGHT	COLOR	REMARKS
Cockscomb *Celosia*	March-September	1-3'	Red, yellow, or- ange, bronze	Showy flower heads of many forms. Dries easily for use in arrangements.
Coreopsis "	September-February	2'	Yellow	Full sun. Good drainage.
Cornflower Bachelor Button *Centaurea cyanus*	September-February	3'	White, blue, pink, purple	Reseeds. Thin for larger plants and flower heads. Blooms best during cool weather.
Cosmos *(Cosmos) Cosmos bipinnatus*	Early February-March	to 5'	Pink, crimson, lavender	Fall-blooming annual. New early blooming varieties available.
Delphinium	September-December	2½'	Blue, pink, lav- ender, white	Sow seeds early. Flowers best cool weather.
Dusty Miller *Cineraria*	March-September	8-10"	Silvery	Excellent contrast plant.
Flowering Cabbage Flowering Kale *Brassica oleracea*	August-November	8-10"	Red, white, pink	Cool weather intensifies color.
Forget-Me-Not *Myosotis Palustria*	October-March	6-10'	Blue	Prefers moist soil, shade. Reseeds.
Geranium	April-September	9-15"	White, pink bicolor, rose, red, pink	Partial shade, good container plant, disease problem, fragrant
Hibiscus *Mallow*	Late spring	3'+	White, yellow, rose, pink, red	Many varieties easily grown. Large, showy flowers up to 6".
Hollyhocks	Spring	4'+	White to pink or purple	Easily grown. Sun.

COMMON NAME	PLANTING TIME	HEIGHT	COLOR	REMARKS
Impatiens *Impatiens sultanas*	April-September	8-18"	Many colors doubles, patterns	Partial shade, shade, well drained, rich soil.
Larkspur *Delphinium spp*	September-February	2-3'	White, blue, purple, pink	Best in cool, moist conditions. Double flowering varieties available.
Lobelia *Lobelia erinus*	November-February	12"	Blue, white	Prefers sunny location. Blooms best during cool spring days.
Lupine *Lupinus spp*	December-March	3'	White, blue, rose	Prefers cool conditions.
Marigold, African *Tagetes spp*	March-July	4-8"	Yellow, orange	Any garden soil. Warm weather plant.
Marigold, French *Tagetes spp*	March-August	12-15"	Yellow, mahogany	Single and double flowers. Sun. Through summer if moisture provided.
Morning Glory *Ipomoca purpurea*	March-May	Vine	White, blue	Vigorous annual vine. Volunteer seedlings of inferior quality.
Nasturtium *Tropacolum minus*	February-April	12-15"	Yellow, red, orange	Over-fertilization will cause excessive vegetative growth.
Pansy *Viola tricolor*	August-November	6-10"	Many colored, splotched and solids	Plants usually live through winter. Flowers in early spring. Prefers rich moist soil.
Periwinkle *Vinca rosea*	March-August	18-20"	White, pink, red	Hot summers. Hardy.
Petunia *Petunia hybrida*	January-March	10-18"	Many colors	Full sun. Partial shade. Single and doubles.
Phlox Annual *Phlox drummondi*	September-March	10-12"	Many colors	Requires abundant moisture. Subject to mildew. Likes extra fertilizer.

COMMON NAME	PLANTING TIME	HEIGHT	COLOR	REMARKS
Pink Dianthus *Dianthus chinensis*	September-February	10-15"	Pink, red, white	Annual or perennial. Fragrant blossoms.
Poppy *Papvaer rholas*	October-December	2-3'	White, cream, red, lavender	Self-seeds in loose, fertile soil. Cool weather flower.
Portulaca Moss Rose *Portulaca grandiflora*	April-July	4-6"	Vari-colored	Rock garden. Hot, dry, poor soil conditions. Flowers open during the morning. Succulent type leaves.
Salvia Scarlet sage *Salvia spendens*	April-September	8"-3'	Red, blue, white	Heat tolerant. Provides excellent color during summer.
Scabiosa Pincushion flower *Scabiosa spp*	September-March	2-3'	White, rose, crimson, blue	Cool weather plant. Stake tall forms.
Snapdragon *Antirrhinum majus*	September-October, January 15-February 15	2-3'	White, pink, red, yellow, bronze	Perennial grown as annual. Dwarfs available. Best under cool conditions.
Spider Plant *Cleome spinosa*	February-May	4-5'	Pink, white, yellow	Reseeds. Easy to grow.
Strawflower *Helichrysum bracteatum*	February-May	3'	White, yellow, orange, red	Cut flowers for drying before fully open.
Sunflower *Helianthus spp*	March-May	4-8'	Yellow	Full sun. Good drainage.

COMMON NAME	PLANTING TIME	HEIGHT	COLOR	REMARKS
Sweet Pea *Lathyrus odoratus*	November-January	3-6'	Vari-colored	Cool weather plant. Prefers soil high in organic matter. Very fragrant.
Verbena *Verbena hybrida*	November-March	Creeping	White, purple, red, blue, pink	Seeds germinate slowly. Sun. Propagated by cuttings.
Zinnia *Zinnia spp*	April-August	24-36"	Vari-colored	Hot, dry locations. Easy to grow. Disease problems.

Chart

Louisiana Cooperative Extension

Perennials

Perennials are plants that do not die after making seeds as do annuals and biennials and live more than three (3) years. Bulbs and ferns are usually considered perennials. As a rule, if it blooms in spring, plant in fall; if it blooms in fall, plant in spring. As with other garden flowers, it is best to keep the spent flowers removed, although this becomes impractical after plants are larger.

Flowers that bloom year after year are a joy in the garden. Use them for accents, for color, and for texture. In your planning, try to have perennials that bloom each season - a succession of color in the landscape. Plant perennials in the front of your flower bed or by themselves to fill a narrow area along a driveway or walk. Few plants give so much pleasure with such little effort.

If you take care in planting them, they will last many years.

Fertilize your plants spring, summer, and fall. To promote flowering, use a high phosphorus fertilizer (e.g. 10-20-10) during the active growth period. If you have a bed with a mixture of flowering and foliage plants, use a balanced fertilizer (e.g. 8-8-8).

PERENNIALS

COMMON NAME	HEIGHT	COLORS	BLOOM TIME	REMARKS
Acanthus *Acanthus mollis*	2-3'	lilac to nearly white (bloom insignificant)	Late spring	Sun. Divide in spring. Large green leaves. Needs winter protection.
Astilbe *Astilbe*	36"	red, white, pink	summer	Moist, well-drained soil.
Bee Balm *Monarda didyma*	24", 36"	pink, scarlet, red, purple daisy like flower	"	Fragrant. Partial shade or sun. Divide in the fall every 2-3 years. Attracts hummingbirds.
Bleeding Heart *Dicentra spectabilis*	2'	white with red centers	early summer	Sun or partial shade.
Garden Chrysanthemum *Chrysanthemums morifolium*	2-4'	white, lavender, brown, yellow, apricot	September, October, early November	Divide after blooms. Sun or partial shade.
Columbine *Aquilegia*	18"	white to blue, yellow to red	spring; early summer	Seeds for new plants.
Coreopsis *Coreopsis grandiflora*	24"	yellow	May	Blooms first year from seed.
Coreopsis auriculata Dwarf	1'	yellow	May	Blooms first year from seed.
Nana *Dwarf C. Tinctoria*	1'	yellow	May	Good in small gardens.

COMMON NAME	HEIGHT	COLORS	BLOOM TIME	REMARKS
Daisy Shasta *Chrysanthemum maximum*	12-24"	white, yellow center	May-June	Divide until June. Likes sun.
Marguerite *Chrysanthemum frutescens*	36"	white	early spring	Divide in spring.
Painted Daisy Pyrethrum *Chrysanthemum coccineum*	12-36"	white, red, rose, pink	summer	Single and double varieties. Sun. Well-drained soil.
Dianthus "Pinks" *Dianthus deltoides*	12"	white, rose, purple	spring-summer	Full sun. Divide in fall.
Four O-Clock *Mirabilis jalapa*	5'	white, yellow, red, lavender, blue	all summer	Sun or partial shade. Can be a pest.
Foxglove *Digitalis purpurea*	4-6'	lavender plus other colors	late spring-summer	Seeds. Sun. Moist, well-drained soil.
Gaillardia Blanketflower *Gaillardia grandiflora*	36"	crimson tipped with yellow or gold	summer	Seeds. Likes sun.
Gerbera Daisy African Daisy *Gerbera Jamesonii*	10"	yellow, coral, pink, orange, red	May to December	Good drainage. Morning sun. Divide in the fall.

COMMON NAME	HEIGHT	COLORS	BLOOM TIME	REMARKS
Helleborus Christmas-rose *H. Niger*	1'	white	winter	Shade.
Lenten-rose *H. Orientalis*	1'	mauve, white	spring	Sun or partial shade. Reseed. Hardy.
Hibiscus *Hibiscus*	6'	from white to deep reds	summer-autumn	Seeds and cuttings. Sun. Protect from freezes.
Hollyhocks *Althea*	9'	pink, rose, purple	spring	Single or double flowered. Sun. Hardy.
Hosta Plantain Lily *Hosta*	1'-3' +	white, blue, lilac. Leaves most valued.	early summer-fall	Divide spring or fall. Does not tolerate hot, dry condition. Do not over fertilize.
Liatris Blazing star Gay-feather *Liatris*	36"	purple, white, rosy purple	summer-early fall	Divide in spring. Sun.
Lupine *Lupinus polyphyllus*	36"	white, pink, yellow, red, blue	April-May	Seeds. Mulch roots to cool in summer.
Blue Bonnet *Lupinus subcarnosus*	8-12"	blue with white or yellow spots	early spring	Seed or divide in spring. Need pH of 7. Most soils need lime.
Oriental Poppy *Papaver Orientale*	24-36"	rosy, salmon, red, lavender, mahogany	spring-summer	Sun. Divide after flowering or by root cutting.
Penstemon *Penstemon*	12-24"	lavender	early spring	Sun or partial shade. Divide in fall or seed in spring.

COMMON NAME	HEIGHT	COLORS	BLOOM TIME	REMARKS
Peony *Paeonia*	18"-3'	red, pink, white	spring	Afternoon shade. Plant in fall. Roots near soil surface. To get maximum color; heavy feeders.

Phlox
  Thrift
  Moss-pink
  Phlox subulata
	4-6'	white, pink, magenta	very early spring	Dry soil, but likes water when in bloom. High maintenance.

Spring Phlox *Phlox divaricata*	10-18"	lavender-blue variation in color	spring	Variety of soils, but prefers moist, rich soil.
Summer Phlox *Phlox paniculata*	36"	white, purple, variation of purple	June into early fall if dead flowers are cut.	Divide in fall every 3 years. Sun or afternoon shade.
Rudbeckia *Rudbeckia*	18"-3'	orange with rust center	spring-frost	Heat, drought tolerant. Good in mass planting.
Scabiosa *Scabiosa caucasica*	30"	blue, white, rich mauve	summer	Divide in spring, or seeds. Sun. Slightly acid, well-drained soil.
Sedum *Sedum acre*	12-18"	yellow—prized, yellow green foliage	spring	Almost any soil. Low maintenance.
Sedum album	12-18"	grey foliage valuable but less vigorous	spring	Almost any soil. Low maintenance. Less vigorous.
Showy sedum *Sedum spectabule*	12-18"	striking foliage	spring	Almost any soil. Low maintenance.

COMMON NAME	HEIGHT	COLORS	BLOOM TIME	REMARKS
Stokesia Stokes' Aster *Stokesia laevis*	10-15"	blue, white, lilac, rosy	May-June	Full sun. Divide in fall.
Verbena *Verbean hybrida*	10-12"	white, pink, red, candy-stripe, lavender, blue	spring, a few into fall	Moist, fertile, well-drained soil. Sun. Divide in the fall. High maintenance.
Violets *Viola odorata*	6-12"	white, pink, violet	early spring	Sun or shade. Divide in the fall.
Yarrow *Achillea Millefolium*	18-24"	white, pink, yellow, valuable foliage	spring-summer	Sun. Hardy. Divide in the fall.

Bulbs

The word "bulbs" is used to describe an assortment of fleshy structures which gardeners plant to obtain various flowering ornamental plants. The beginning gardener and many experienced growers as well do not differentiate between bulbs, corms, tubers, rhizomes, and certain other plant structures used to propagate plants. This is a cause of confusion for more seasoned gardeners who are more particular as to what "planting bulbs in your garden" really means.

All gardeners should strive to learn about the plants they grow. Becoming aware of the individual plant growth behavior is as fascinating as seeing your garden in full flower. The full experience of gardening can afford one a lifetime of reward and pleasure, so let us look more closely at the distinguishing features of bulbs:

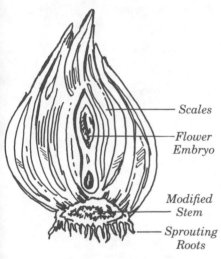

Scales

Flower Embryo

Modified Stem

Sprouting Roots

CROSS-SECTION OF A BULB

BULBS ARE STRUCTURES MADE UP OF A MASS OF OVERLAPPING LAYERS OR SCALES. These scales arise from a modified stem at the base. Roots start to form as the bulb completes a rest period (dormancy) and the flower embryo begins to shoot upward and arise as a bud and then open into the glorious flowers we have long awaited.

Examples of Ornamental Bulbs: Narcissus (Daffodils), Tulips, Dutch Hyacinths, Amaryllis, Crinums, and true Lilies are among some of the popular garden bulbs.

One could spend many months delving into information about each bulb-type plant and find intricate classifications that lend to further identifying characteristics which make for more detailed knowledge. Many gardeners will take an interest in one particular type of bulb, such as Narcissus, and learn the many types, names, and identities, as well as experience the fun and knowledge of growing each.

The basics of growing bulbs can be as simple or detailed as the extent of your interest in the use of bulbs in your garden. If your garden is not a favorite place to spend your free moments, then you may only choose to plant a few bulbs here and there to naturalize or form

"clumps" over the years without any further attention than necessary to control weeds around them. Other gardeners choose to treat their bulbs as annuals and plant them for their season of bloom, then dig them and place them in another location as outlying fence line plantings; some even give them away or throw them away. Bulbs lend themselves to any form of planting arrangement. They can be used to give quite formal design plantings arranged in masses of individual colors and combinations of colors to form intricate designs and displays as in the elegant formal European gardens. Enthusiastic gardeners may utilize bulbs in and among any combination of plants of many colors and flower types, as in the noted English cottage gardens. Their use is suitable for every purpose. We have only to select the proper types, colors, and sizes to fill our needs. We also must pay particular attention to the season of bloom, for there are bulbs for every season.

The beginner may find it best to venture into the use of bulbs on a "trial and error" basis, but also may seek out guidance from good gardeners, gardening books, and other literature which is available at the Agriculture Extension Service, libraries, or garden clubs. Unfortunately, there will always be a good bit of misinformation in some publications as geographic and climatic conditions vary a good bit from one city to another and even from one garden to another. These variations make it difficult to have accurate information available to guide you. Experience will always prove to be your best teacher!

As a rule of thumb, bulbs are seen on the market at garden centers at the ideal planting time. Spring flowering bulbs can be found advertised during the fall months and conversely. This is the best cue for the beginner to be reminded to prepare the planting areas and proceed with the planting of bulbs. It is also the time for gardeners to dig up and divide plantings of the same type of bulbs being marketed which they have had for three or more years in their gardens. The divisions may be planted in new locations to give more plantings of that type of bulb.

The major planting periods in a garden occur in the fall and spring. It is difficult to say if these are the times when the weather is more inviting to work in the garden, but generally the weather is more complementary to planting during these seasons. Once flower beds have been disturbed and soil loosened to incorporate fertilizers and organic material, several good soaking rains are needed to settle the beds back into the natural system whereby plants can draw moisture from the soil. Fall and spring are the only times we are certain to have recurring gentle rains to restore this vital process.

A multitude of questions are sure to remain as a beginner embarks upon planting bulbs. How deep to plant them? Where to place each

type? How far apart should one bulb be from the next bulb? Much of this will come with experience, for there are no absolute rules that apply to all types of bulbs. Often the size of the bulb you are about to plant will be an indicator of the amount of space you need to allow between bulbs. Large bulbs usually yield large bouquets of flowers, but some will fool you and will have to be moved to another location. Some brave souls do this when the plant is in full bloom, and by careful watering and tending are able to enjoy the results. Other gardeners have a system of digging and coding bulbs after they bloom for planting at the end of the season, or a system of drying them and waiting until planting time the following season.

Once bulbs bloom they often leave an unsightly display of drying foliage which gardeners sometimes try to hide by tying the foliage back or cutting it off. It is important that a good portion of the foliage be allowed to die back naturally so that the bulb can take in the food supply it needs to restore the bulb's vigor. Once the bulb has taken in this supply of food, it goes into a resting state, or dormancy. On certain bulbs such as daffodils (Narcissus), this occurs during the summer months and is a time for gardeners to let them dry out by withholding watering until fall planting time, at which time one incorporates fertilizer and organic additives to trigger the end of dormancy and initiate root growth and flower bud formation.

A beginning gardener is likely to have selected some plant that grows from a bulb at a very early stage in her selection of plants, for bulbs have great appeal to gardeners and non-gardeners alike. The real treasure of bulbs is their ease of care and their profusion of blooms which only get better and better with each gardening season. Additionally, many bulbs bear flowers with fragrances that enchant us, either as specimens in the garden or as cut flowers indoors. One can never learn enough about bulbs nor cease to enjoy them. The planting of bulbs can make for a fascinating hobby and study.

Article prepared by
Joan A. Pitcher
Grandaughter of Mrs. U.B. Evans
Nationally known horticulturist
Haphazard Plantation, Ferriday, LA

Tip: Before planting bulbs, shake in a bag with baby powder or medicated powder to discourage squirrels.

BULBS (B), CORMS (C), RHIZOMES (R), TUBERS (T), AND TUBEROUS ROOTS (TR)

All of these are commonly called bulbs. Most like a sunny location in a neutral to slightly acid (pH 6-7), well-drained soil. When planting new bulbs or transplanting old ones, work a high phosphorus fertilizer (e.g. 10-20-10) into a permanent bed. If bulbs are to be treated as annuals (e.g. tulips and caladiums), no fertilizer is needed.

Use a high phosphorus fertilizer in your established bulb bed when you see the green foliage emerging. This will promote better bloom for the current season and encourage food storage for future seasons. Fertilize again after blooming.

Flowers should be "deadheaded," but the foliage should be left on until it dries to provide food for the bulb's growth and vitality.

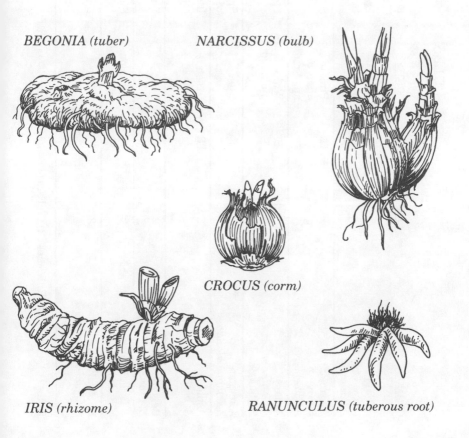

BEGONIA (tuber)

NARCISSUS (bulb)

CROCUS (corm)

IRIS (rhizome)

RANUNCULUS (tuberous root)

BULBS

COMMON NAME BOTANICAL NAME	PLANT DEPTH	TYPE	COLORS	BLOOM TIME	REMARKS
Allium Giant Onion *Allium*	4"	B	Lavender, white, yellow	Spring, summer. Some are 4" across.	Sun. Good cut flower.
Alstroemeria Peruvian Lily *Alstroemeria*	2"	TR	Pink to orange, orange-red	Summer	Good cut flower. Can be a weed.
Amaryllis A. *Belladonna* Belladonna Lily	Up to the neck	B	White, pink, red	Spring	Not hardy. Sun. Good container plant.
Anemone *Anemone blandas*	1 or 2"	T	Blue	Spring, late winter	Sun or partial shade. Good strains are de Caen & St. Brigid.
Aspidistra A. *elatior*	2"	TB	Green foliage	Inconspicuous bloom	Hardy. Good container plant. Shade or partial shade. Heat resistant. Also a variegated variety.
Begonia Hardy *B. grandis*	2"	T	Pink	Winter-fall	Semi-tuberous. Partial shade.
B. Tuberous *B. Tuber hybrida*	2"	T	All colors except blue	Summer	Showy flowers. Many varieties.
Butterfly Lily *Hedychium coronarium*	2"	R	White	Late summer-fall	Fragrant. Blooms resemble butterflies. Water freely. Sun or shade.

Bulbs (B), Corms (C), Rhizomes (R), Tubers (T), and Tuberous Roots (TR)

COMMON NAME BOTANICAL NAME	PLANT DEPTH	TYPE	COLORS	BLOOM TIME	REMARKS
Caladium *Caladium hortulanum*	2"	T	Decorative colorful leaves—red pink, white, variegated	Bloom not desired as much as leaves. Summer	Good for beds or containers. Store bulbs over winter. Likes shade and water.
Calla Lily *Zantedeschia*	2"	C	Yellow, white	Early spring	Sun or partial shade.
Cannas *Canna*	2"	R	Yellow, pink, orange, scarlet	Summer to frost	Sun. Likes rich soil.
Chionodoxa *Glory-of-the-Snow*	2 to 3"	B	White, pink	Late winter	Good to naturalize. Sun.
Colchicum *Colchicum*	2 to 3"	C	Pink, lavender, white	Autumn	Sun or partial shade. Fragrant.
Crinum Lily *Crinum*	3-6"	B	White, pink, red	Summer	Sun or partial shade.
Crocus *Crocus*	2"	B	Purple, lilac, white, yellow, striped	Winter	Naturalize
Daffodil (See article, pg. 127)					

Bulbs (B), Corms (C), Rhizomes (R), Tubers (T), and Tuberous Roots (TR)

COMMON NAME BOTANICAL NAME	TYPE	COLORS	BLOOM TIME	PLANT DEPTH	REMARKS
Dahlia *Dahlia*	B	All colors	Summer & fall	2"	Good for cutting.
Daylily *Hemerocallis*	TR	All colors	Spring-Summer	2-3"	Water freely. Hardy. Good planted in masses and colors grouped.
Gladiolus *Gladiolus*	C	Many colors	Spring-summer	2"	Good cut flowers. Sun or partial shade. Good in masses. Hardy. Sun or shade.
Gloriosa *Gloriosa*	T	Red, yellow, orange	Spring-summer	4"	Sun. Vine. Needs good support.
Hyacinth *Hyancinthus*	B	White, pink, blue, yellow, orange, lavender	Spring	5"	Plant annually. Water freely. Fragrant.
Roman Hyacinth	B	White, pink, blue	Early spring	5"	Fragrant. Plant annually.
Iris Bearded Many varieties	R	All colors	Spring	1"	Alkaline soil, sun. Good drainage. Slightly acid soil, sun, partial shade. Cut leaves in fan shape when brown at the tip.
Crested *I Cristata I Japonica I Tectoram*	R	Blue, white, lavender	late spring, late summer	1" or less	"

Bulbs (B), Corms (C), Rhizomes (R), Tubers (T), and Tuberous Roots (TR)

COMMON NAME BOTANICAL NAME	PLANT DEPTH	TYPE	COLORS	BLOOM TIME	REMARKS
Dutch	3"	B	White, blue, yellow	Spring	Sun, well drained soil.
Japanese *Kaempferi*	1"	R	White, purple	Late spring	Partial shade. Acid soil.
Louisiana Several species	1"–5"	R	White, pink, red, yellow, blue, purple, bronze	Spring	Sun-partial shade. Keep mulched. Acid soil.
Reticulata *I Reticulata*	4"	R	Violet	Winter	Fragrant. Short stem bloom. Moist soil. Leave undistrubed.
Siberian *I Siberica*	1"	R	Blue, purple	Spring	"
Ismene or Peruvian Daffodil *Hymenocallis calathina*	4"	B	White	Late Spring	Sandy soil. Water freely. Sun. Very fragrant.
Lily *Lilium Hybrid*	4-6"	B	Many colors	Spring to summer	Plant in sun or partial shade. Well drained soil. Excellent cut flower. Most fragrant.
Ace, Easter, Creole *L. Longiflorium*	4-6"	B	White	Early Spring	Plant in sun or partial shade. Well drained soil. Excellent cut flower. Most fragrant.

Bulbs (B), Corms (C), Rhizomes (R), Tubers (T), and Tuberous Roots (TR)

73

COMMON NAME BOTANICAL NAME	TYPE	COLORS	BLOOM TIME	PLANT DEPTH	REMARKS
Madonna *L. Candidum*	B	White	Late spring	3-4"	Plant in sun or partial shade. Well drained soil. Excellent cut flower. Most fragrant.
Regal *L. Regal*	B	White, pink, spots	Mid spring	4-6"	"
Rubrum *L. Speciosum*	B	White to rose, pink	Late spring	4-6"	"
Lily of the Valley *Convallaria*	R	White	Spring	1"	Not too hardy. May be forced. Fragrant.
Lycoris Golden Spider Lily *L. Africana*	B	Yellow	Summer	3-4"	Blooms before foliage appears. Sun. Feed when foliage appears.
Spider Lily or Naked Lady *L. Radiata*	B	Red	Late summer	3-4"	"
Resurrection Lily *L. Squamigera*	B	Pink	Summer	5"	"
Montbretia *Tritonia*	C	Orange to scarlet	Summer	1"	Sun or shade. Water sparingly. Good cut flower.
Narcissus: (See section on Daffodils)					
Oxalis *Oxalis*	B	Pink, yellow	Spring	1"	Naturalizes. Good for border, rock gardens.
Scilla *Endymion Hispanicus*	B	White, pink, blue	Spring	1-2"	Sun to shade.

Bulbs (B), Corms (C), Rhizomes (R), Tubers (T), and Tuberous Roots (TR)

COMMON NAME BOTANICAL NAME	PLANT DEPTH	TYPE	COLORS	BLOOM TIME	REMARKS
Snowdrops *Galanthus Nivalis*	1-2"	B	White	Winter	Partial shade.
Snowflake *Leucojum aestivum*	1-2"	B	White, green dot on rim	Winter-spring	Sandy, loam soil. Partial shade. Naturalizes.
Tulip *Tulipa*	4" clay soil 6" sandy soil	B	Many pleasing colors	Early spring Mid spring Late spring varieties	Best treated as annuals. Sun or part shade. Protect from spring wind damage to flowers. Buy when first in the market, then refrigerate. Good container grown. Good cut flower. Late spring ones good in Zone 8.
Watsonia *Watsonia*	3"	C	Many	Spring	Good cut flower. Same culture as gladiolus.
Zephyranthes Rain Lily *Z. ajax, Z candida, Z. citrina, Z. grandiflora*	2"	B	Yellow, white, gold, pink	Summer-fall	Sun or shade. Good in small gardens. Naturalizes. Water freely.

Bulbs (B), Corms (C), Rhizomes (R), Tubers (T), and Tuberous Roots (TR)

Shrubs

A shrub, according to Webster, is a low, many-stemmed woody plant as opposed to the small tree which is a one trunk plant.

No one denies the importance of the stately tree or green lawn, but the shrub is the plant to bring it all together. It is transitional – the very heart of the landscape design. Evergreen or deciduous, each shrub has its own value. The evergreen shrub offers year round beauty as a foundation planting; background for colorful annuals, perennials, or bulb beds; or hedges for privacy or screening. There is a shrub for beauty in all seasons whether the beauty lies in its flowers, berries, or even its bare branches.

Some considerations in the selection of shrubs are these:

Know your site and the needs to be met.

Be sure to buy from a reliable source.

Never buy at random. Shape and make beds before purchasing so you will know size, function, etc.

A larger plant may be a better investment even at higher cost. You will need fewer plants and see instantly if it meets your needs.

A soil test will let you know specifically what fertilizer is needed and the exact amount, but generally, shrubs may be fed as follows:

Spring flowering shrubs – a fertilizer high in phosphorous (e.g. 10-20-10) in the summer to foster good bud set and bloom. Following bloom, feed again with a balanced fertilizer (e.g. 13-13-13).

Summer flowering shrubs – a balanced fertilizer as signs of growth appear in early spring and again after they have bloomed.

Evergreens – a fertilizer high in nitrogen (e.g. 16-8-8) before new spring growth, then in late spring, and in early fall.

Acid-loving plants such as azaleas, camellias, hydrangeas, and gardenias respond best to special fertilizers designed for them.

To maintain healthy, beautiful shrubs, follow a schedule for fertilizing, spraying for disease and pests, watering, pruning, and replacing mulch.

SHRUBS

COMMON NAME BOTANICAL NAME	DECIDUOUS or EVERGREEN	LIGHT REQUIREMENTS	HEIGHT	REMARKS
Abelia *Abelia grandiflora*	E	Sun. Partial shade.	6-8'	Upright, spreading form. Pest free. White, pinkish flowers. Green in summer; reddish in fall.
Almond (flowering) *Prunus glandulosa*	D	Sun	4'	Pink pom-pom like blossoms on bare branch. Upright form.
Althea *Hibiscus*	D	Sun	15'	Large blooms if pruned. Pink, purple, or white. Single or double flowers.
Aucuba *Aucuba*	E	Partial Shade	8'	Rounded form. Large showy leaves. Flowers in winter.
Azalea (See section on Azaleas)				
Banana Shrub *Michelia Figo*	E	Sun. Partial shade.	6'+	Tree-like. Fragrant.
Barberry Winter Green Barberry *Berberis Julianae*	E	Sun	4-6'	Dense, spine barrier. Oval-round.
Berberis Thunbergii	D	Sun	4'	Red-purple fall foliage. Oval.
Beautyberry French Mulberry *Callicarpa americana*	D	Shade, sun	6-8'	Stands drought. Native plant. Purple berries in early fall. Spreading form.
Beauty Bush *Kolkwitzia amabilis*	D	Sun	6-16'	White flower clusters.

77

COMMON NAME BOTANICAL NAME	DECIDUOUS or EVERGREEN	LIGHT REQUIREMENTS	HEIGHT	REMARKS

Boxwood
  Korean Boxwood
  Buxus microphylla
	E	Sun. Partial shade.	3'	Upright. Disease problems.

English Box *Buxus sempervirens*	E	Partial shade. Sun.	3-5'	Upright. Problems.
Buckeye *Aesculus pavia*	E	Sun. Partial shade.	10-12'	Spreading form. Red flowers.
Camellia (See section on Camellias)				
Cleyera *Cleyera japonica*	E	Sun or partial shade.	6'+	Glossy dark green foliage.
Cotoneaster *Cotoneaster apiculatus*	D	Sun	18-24"	Dense growth. Good drainage. Red berries.
Deutzia *Deutzia gracilis*	D	Sun	6'+	Mounded shape. Snowy white or pink flowers.
Elderberry	D	Sun	12-15'	White flowers, then black berries. Favorite of birds. Good for wine, jam, and pie.
Elaeagnus *Elaeagnus angustiflora*	E	Partial shade. Sun.	8'	Oval growth pattern.
E. pungens	E	Sun. Partial shade.	8'	Oval, graceful, arching.
Euonymus *Euonymus patens*	Semi-E	Sun	3-6'	Spreading form. Dark green foliage.
Euonymus americanas	E	Sun, Shade.	3-6'	Native Louisiana plant. Pest free.

COMMON NAME BOTANICAL NAME	DECIDUOUS or EVERGREEN	LIGHT REQUIREMENTS	HEIGHT	REMARKS
E. japonica microphylla	E	Sun	6-24"	Dwarf compact like boxwood.
E. fortunei	E	Sun	3-6'	Trailing, climbing. 2" leaves.
Fatsia *Fatsia japonica*	E	Shade	4-8'	Ball like heads of white flowers. Large glossy leaf.
Forsythia *Forsythia intermedia*	D	Sun	6-8'	Yellow flowers. Many varieties. Do not prune into a bud. Prune old canes to the ground.
French Mulberry *Callicarpa americana*	D	Sun, Shade	6-8'	Magenta or white cluster of berries. Stands drought.
Gardenia *Gardenia jasminoides*	E	Sun or light shade	6'+	Round form. Large fragrant flowers. Several varieties that bloom spring, summer, fall. Good container plant.
Holly *Ilex* Dwarf Chinese	E	Sun	3'	Mounded. Dependable small shrub.
I. Helleri	E	Sun	3'	Spreading. One of the best small leaf hollies.
Burford	E	Sun	6'+	Oval form. Brilliant red berries. Male and female on the same plant.
Possum Haw *Decidua*	D	Sun	6'+	Upright. Spreading. Outstanding red fruit. Pest free. Needs male pollination.

COMMON NAME BOTANICAL NAME	DECIDUOUS or EVERGREEN	LIGHT REQUIREMENTS	HEIGHT	REMARKS
Foster's	E	Sun	6' +	Upright. Oval.
Inkberry or Winterberry	E	Sun, partial shade	6' +	Black berries. Disease and insect free.
Yaupon *I. vomitoria*	E	Sun. Partial shade.	6-15'	Small red or yellow berries. Excellent shrub. Pest free. Fast growing. Topiaries easily. Upright or weeping form.
Honeysuckle, Winter *Lonicera fragratissima*	E	Sun	6-8'	Spicy, fragrant, creamy white flowers. Many varieties. Any soil. Pest free.
Huckleberry *Vaccinum virgatum*	D	Sun, shade	3-6'	Flowers in spring, fruit in summer. Oval, round form. Nice fall color.
Hydrangea (see section on Hydrangeas)				
Jasmine *Jasminum humile*	E	Partial shade. Sun	6' +	Arching form. Bright yellow flowers.
Winter Jasmine *Jasminum nudifloram*	D	Sun	6' +	Oval. Yellow blossoms on bare branches.
Jasminum floridum	Semi-E	Sun	3-6'	Showy yellow flowers. Mounded form. Dense. Pest free. Good for banks and slopes.

COMMON NAME BOTANICAL NAME	DECIDUOUS or EVERGREEN	LIGHT REQUIREMENTS	HEIGHT	REMARKS
Juniper *Juniper horizonatalis Douglasii*	E	Partial shade	6-11"	Spreading form. Used as ground cover. Color change. Steel blue. Stands hot, dry conditions.
Juniperus h. procumbens	E	Sun	6-11"	Dark green foliage. Creeping, spreading. Very dwarf.
Juniperus h. plumosa	E	Sun	4-11"	Spreading, compact. Purplish in fall. Feathery foliage.
Juniperus h. 'Bar Harbour'	E	Sun	6-11"	Blue-green in summer; bronze in winter. Creeping, spreading. Compact. One of the best ground covers.
Juniperus sabina Tamaris-cifolia	E	Sun	6-11"	One of the best. Bright green foliage. Grey selections available.
Blue vase *Juniperus chinensis*	E	Sun	6-8'	Steel blue foliage. Massive shaggy form. Red spider a problem.
Juniperus chinensis sylvestris	E	Sun	6'+	Conical form. Good for dense screen. Red spider a problem.
Kerria *Kerria Japonica*	D	Semi-shade	8'	Neat. Slender growth. Single strong yellow flower. Dark green foliage.
Lantana Shrub verbena *Lantana Camara Hybrid*	Semi-E	Sun	6'	Many colored flowers. Spreading form. Not too hardy.

COMMON NAME / BOTANICAL NAME	DECIDUOUS or EVERGREEN	LIGHT REQUIREMENTS	HEIGHT	REMARKS
Laurel Cherry Laurel *Prunus laurocerasus*	E	Sun, shade	12'	Tree form. Can be used as a hedge.
Ligustrum *Ligustrum Japonicum*	E	Sun, shade	12'	Upright tree form. Fast growing. Requires pruning. Subject to white fly. Dense green foliage.
Privet *Ligustrum vulgare*	E	Sun, Partial shade	10-15'	Many kinds grown for foliage. Dense screen.
Mahonia *Mahonia beale*	E	Sun, Partial shade	6' +	Yellow flowers in spring, followed by blue fruit. Holly like foliage. Bluish color.
Oregon Grape *M. aquifolium*	E	Sun. Partial shade.	6'	Upright form. Good blue-green holly like foliage. Young foliage reddish.
M. fortunei	E	Shade, Semi-shade	4-6'	Irregular oval. Fern-like leaves. Yellow flowers in spring. Blue berries in winter.
Mock Orange English dogwood *Philadelphus*	D	Sun	12'	Upright, spreading. Fragrant white flowers in spring.
Nandina Heavenly bamboo *Nandina domestica*	E	Sun	3-8'	Small white flowers. Red berries. Bronze to red foliage in spring. Very desirable. Prune by thinning. Nice in containers.
N. domestica nana purpurea	E	Sun	12-19"	Dwarf. Thick foliage. Red to purplish bronze. Very hardy.

COMMON NAME BOTANICAL NAME	DECIDUOUS or EVERGREEN	LIGHT REQUIREMENTS	HEIGHT	REMARKS
Oleander *Nerium oleander*	E	Sun	6'+	Many colors. Upright form. One of best summer flowering shrubs. Subject to scale.
Osmanthus Sweet Olive *O. fragrans*	E	Sun, Partial shade	20'	Upright form. Cluster of small white flowers. Very fragrant. Slow growth. Pest free.
Pearl Bush *Exochorda racemosa*	D	Sun	6-10'	Upright form. Showy white flowers.
Pieris *Pieris japonica*	E	Partial shade	6'	Compact. Spreading, drooping panicles. Showy white flowers.
Photinia *Photinia glabra*	E	Sun	6-10"	Red spiny foliage. Upright form.
Pineapple quava *Feijoa sellowiana*	E	Sun or partial shade	6-10'	Round form. Leaf light green, silver back.
Pittosporum *Pittosporum tobira*	E	Sun to shade	6-8'	Mound form. Fragrant cluster. Very white flowers. Also a variegated one. A good screening plant.
Podocarpus Japanese Yew *P. macrophylla "maki"*	E	Sun or partial shade	10'+	Conical form. Good for narrow area. Aphids love it. A conifer.
Pomegranate *Punica granatum*	D	Sun	6-10'	Flame colored double flowers followed by edible fruit. Pest free. Upright form.
Pyracantha *Pyrancantha coccinea*	E	Sun	6-15'	Spreading form. Red berries in winter.

83

COMMON NAME / BOTANICAL NAME	DECIDUOUS or EVERGREEN	LIGHT REQUIREMENTS	HEIGHT	REMARKS
P. coccinea lalandi	E	Sun	6-15'	Orange berries. Very hardy. Subject to pests.
Quince Cydonia obonga	D	Sun	2-8'	Red flower. Upright form. Blooms on bare branches in late winter.
Chaenomeles lagenaria	D	Sun	2-8'	White, pink, scarlet, red flowers. Can be forced.
Raphiolepis Indian hawthorn Raphiolepis umbellata	E	Sun	3-6'	Clusters of fragrant pink flowers. Dark blue berries.
Rhododendron Rhododendron	D or E	Shade	3-6'	Fragrant. All colors.
Spiraea Bridal wreath Spiraea cantoniensis	D	Sun	6-8'	Arching form. Showy white flowers in early spring. Single or double. Often called Reevesiana.
Bridal wreath S. Pruniflora	D	Sun	6'	Upright form. Double white flowers. Easy to grow.
S. Thunbergi	D	Sun	5'	Upright form. Leaves turn orange in fall. White flowers. Slender, graceful branches. Fruit in fall.
Viburnum Viburnum burkwoodii	E	Sun	4-6'	Round clusters of pink or white star-shaped flowers. Fragrant. Red to black berries. Dark red fall foliage which remains late.

COMMON NAME BOTANICAL NAME	DECIDUOUS or EVERGREEN	LIGHT REQUIREMENTS	HEIGHT	REMARKS
V. carlesii	D	Sun	5'	Most fragrant pink and white clusters of flowers. Dark green foliage.
V. carlcephalum	D	Sun	6-7'	Upright form. Fragrant ball-shaped clusters of white star-shaped flowers. Red to black berries. Red fall foliage. Strong grower. Fragrant. "Snowball."
V. japonicum	E	Sun	8'+	Upright form. Large glossy green leaves. Fast growing. Pest free.
V. macrocephalum	Semi-E	Sun or shade	7-12'	Upright form. Large snowball clusters of white flowers.
V. macrophyllum	E	Sun or partial shade	8-10'	Excellent foliage quality. Fragrant white flowers. Red berries.
V. odoratissimum	E	Sun or partial shade	12'	Excellent foliage quality. White, fragrant spring flowers. Excellent screen. Pest-free. Rapid grower. Fruit red becoming black.
Old Fashioned Snowball V. opulus	D	Sun or partial shade	12'	Large showy clusters of white flowers followed by scarlet juicy fruit. Vigorous grower. Subject to aphids. Upright. Oval.
V. suspensum	E	Sun or partial shade	12'	Mound form. Smaller coarse foliage. More compact grower than some other viburnums. Fragrant pinkish spring flowers.

COMMON NAME / BOTANICAL NAME	DECIDUOUS or EVERGREEN	LIGHT REQUIREMENTS	HEIGHT	REMARKS
Vitex Chaste-Tree *Vitext agnus-castus*	D	Sun	8-10'	Upright form. Large panicles of li-lac flowers. Grey-green foliage with pungent odor.
Wax Myrtle *Myrica cerifera*	E	Sun, partial shade	10' +	Upright, spreading dark green ar-omatic foliage. Good in wet areas.
Weigela *Weigela florida*	D	Sun, shade	8-10'	Pink-rose flowers in spring.
W. floribunda	D	Sun, Shade	8-10'	Upright, spreading form. Red flowers.
S. Vanhouttei	D	Sun	6'	Upright form. White single flowers.
S. bumalda	D	Sun	3-5'	Pink-deep rose flowers in late spring.
Yaupon (see Holly)				
Yew *Traxus*	E	Sun, Partial shade	12' +	Good hedge planting. Ornamental plant or excellent container plant.

Special note from the Crape Myrtle city: This deciduous plant is in many colors and sizes from hanging baskets, dwarf (less than 3') to trees (over 25').

Trees

A royal tree has left us royal fruit, . . .
Shakespeare - *RICHARD III*

Trees are magic. Whether or not you believe that the Good Fairies still live in them is immaterial, because when you view the foliage on a tree or note the erect posture of its trunk, you know that you are in the presence of royalty, so give careful consideration to a tree that you select to put in your garden. There are some things that you need to know, such as the size of the tree at maturity. Is it evergreen or deciduous? Does it have the genes to help it withstand disease and adverse conditions? Will the foliage be as attractive in the house to celebrate the seasons as it is in the yard for the birds to enjoy? Trees are planted for many reasons. Educate yourself about yours and don't be disappointed.

This area of the South has a long growing season and soil that would make almost any plant thrive. No one tree is considered the most suitable, but where it is to be placed is of prime importance. It should not be crowded. A Yew or a Water Oak would give quietness and elegance to the front (public) landscape, while a flowering or berried tree would be a pleasant sight outside a bedroom window which is usually in the back (private) garden.

Trees of different height, shape, and color add character to your landscape. Many times the native Magnolia grandiflora occupies a prominent location in a garden. This tree has a creamy white bloom

| PYRAMIDAL | CONICAL | COLUMNAR | SPREADING |

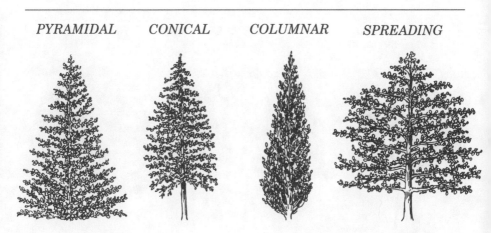

which is perfect for the graduate or bridal bouquet. If this tree is too large, try the Sweet Bay Magnolia; it is on a smaller scale and has the same bloom on gray-green foliage. Loquat is another small native that could be included in the plan of the yard. It has an interesting bark that makes a nice background for the large leathery leaves. The holly trees, particularly the American Holly, do splendidly outside and inside. The birds like the red berries, and the leaves last a long time when they are cut for the house.

Among other trees worth considering is the Tallow, sometimes called a Popcorn tree because of its white berries. Its foliage often provides a brilliant fall color. The limbs can be cut with long stems for a vase, or the berries may be fashioned into a wreath for the entrance or the dining table. If they are properly conditioned, the branches hold their dignity for many seasons. The River Birch has graceful lines and a reddish bark that darkens with age. It is a charming native that will do well either near the water, its natural habitat, or close to the house amid a bed of wildflowers. Do plant some Crape Myrtles for their lovely summer bloom as well as for their beautiful bare winter branches. The bark grows more interesting as it whitens with age. Monroe, Louisiana, has been designated Crape Myrtle City, and both visitors and local residents enjoy the lovely specimens that have been planted. The Bradford Pear has exquisite form and is a spectacular sight in the spring when it is covered with white blooms. It is a fine accent tree when planted in front of a dark green background. Redbuds and Dogwoods are awe-inspiring sights in their spring flowering, but they sometimes have to be replaced because of their short life span. Crabapples and Mayhaws are planted for their fruit and the English Hawthorn for its fragrance. The Cypress and Ginkgo have nice forms

VASE-SHAPED   *WEEPING*   *ROUNDED*

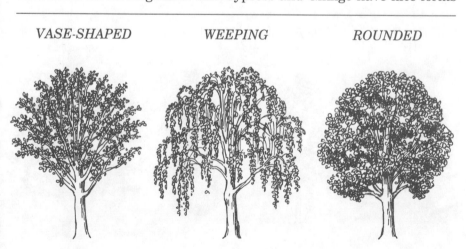

and glorious coloring in the fall. Through the years, the trees in your garden will give you more pleasure than you received when you set them in the ground.

Trees may be planted anytime if they are kept watered, but the easiest time to plant is in December, January, or February. After the fall rains, the soil is more friable, and the root system can become better established before the new growth of spring.

There are two ways to plant a tree: bare rooted or balled.

To plant a bare rooted tree, first soak it in a tub for 24 hours. Dig a hole the size and depth to hold the root system. Set the tree in the hole and surround it with part of the excavated dirt to which humus has been added. Water and then pack the remainder of the dirt around the tree. Water to keep the roots from drying out until the tree becomes acclimated to its home. A bare rooted tree is usually cheaper, and it develops a strong root system. Only small trees are suitable for this method.

Set a balled tree in a hole that is sufficient to hold the burlap in which it is encased. Set the tree in the hole; open the burlap, pushing it to the bottom of the hole; and return some of the soil (with added humus), filling in around the tree. Water, finish putting the dirt around the tree, and water again.

To transplant a tree, follow the same procedure - except that about 2 months before removal, it should be root-pruned. To do this, dig in a circle around the tree, deep enough to cut and shorten the roots. Cutting 18-24" apart will leave enough of the root system so that when the tree is put in the new location, the roots are able to adjust. For example, for a small tree root prune about 3-4 feet from the trunk; for a larger tree, about 6 feet. (For an alternate method, see Summer: It's Time to Prune.)

However, if the tree exceeds 2 or 3 inches in trunk diameter, the soil ball will be heavy and difficult to move intact. This job is probably best left to professionals with power equipment. Thinning a transplanted tree is recommended to reduce water loss until roots grow out.

Avoid planting trees near or under utility wires or where roots will cause damage, such as near sidewalks, driveways, or patios, etc.

Spring is fertilizing time. Here are some methods of feeding your trees:

Surface fertilizing is done by sprinkling or spreading food in a circle around a tree at the drip line. This is best done before a drenching rain because the fertilizer must be watered well.

Foliar feeding is done by a jar attached to the hose. The water-diluted fertilizer coats the foliage of the tree.

Root plug feeding is done by drilling holes about 8-10" deep every 18-24" in a circle around the tree at the drip line. Put dry or liquid fertilizer in the holes. Cover with dirt and water.

How do you make your tree look royal? Learn the art of pruning. Pruning can either destroy your tree or make it into a majestic one. Flat tops and box shapes should be avoided unless you are planning to shape the tree into a topiary or to espalier it against a wall. Graceful lines should be maintained at all times. The different lengths of the branches should hold beauty, whether they are filled with foliage or bared by winter's frost. Long or short but never bowed in, limbs swaying with the wind are dancers.

Never prune in late summer or early fall as new growth might be stimulated which an early frost would kill.

Fall-berried plants should be tip-pruned only along the new growth, but prune out dead wood anytime.

Black film, bag worms, and other problems must be treated. The Epiphytes - such as moss, orchids, and the resurrection fern - are not harmful. They are not parasites but use the tree for structural support.

It is an excellent idea to check with the Agricultural Extension Service. Their experts have the latest information on the care and cultivation of anything that grows. They are generous with their help and will not only analyze your soil, but tell you how to improve it. If your tree is ill, they will identify the disease and advise you on treating it. Their service is invaluable, and in consulting them you will be rewarded with more beautiful trees.

Remembering that yours is a royal tree, plant it carefully, tend it throughout the winter, so that in the spring and summer you will find not only royal fruit, but the fruits of the Spirit that St. Paul speaks of: love, joy, peace, gentleness, goodness, and faith.

How a Tree Grows

Trees increase each year in height and spread of branches by adding on a new growth of twigs.

Leaves make food for the tree by combining carbon dioxide from the air and water from the soil in the presence of sunlight. This process is called photosynthesis.

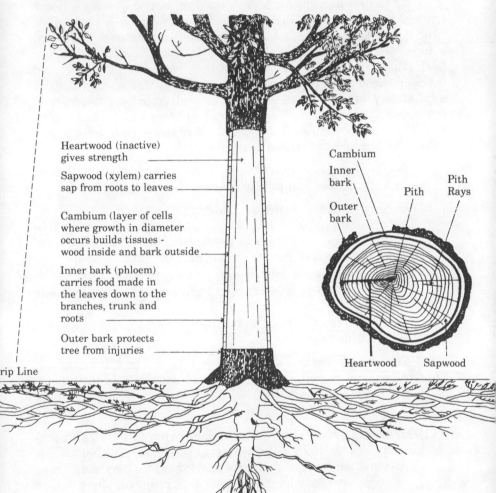

Heartwood (inactive) gives strength

Sapwood (xylem) carries sap from roots to leaves

Cambium (layer of cells where growth in diameter occurs builds tissues - wood inside and bark outside

Inner bark (phloem) carries food made in the leaves down to the branches, trunk and roots

Outer bark protects tree from injuries

Drip Line

Cambium

Inner bark

Outer bark

Pith

Pith Rays

Heartwood

Sapwood

Roots located in the upper 12" - 18" of soil take up water containing small quantities of minerals in solution.

91

Lawns

*A garden is a moving, growing entity, and to maintain it in a
particular style is an evergrowing discipline.*

John Brooks

There is nothing quite so pleasing to the eye as a home
framed by a beautiful, lush green carpet of grass. A term often
used to describe such a setting is "well-manicured." This, of
course, brings to mind a lawn which is edged, trimmed, mowed to
perfection, weedless, and beautiful in color. It is easier and
quicker these days to maintain such a beautiful scene with the
availability of new lawn equipment - electric or gas-powered
trimmers, "weed-eaters," edgers, riding mowers, blowers, etc.,
etc., etc.! And to think all these and more have replaced a hoe, a
rake, and the old-timey push reel mower!

To establish such a scene, the new home gardener will need
to begin with proper soil preparation:

Grading to provide proper drainage
Testing samples of soil for its pH factor. This should be 6.0-
7.0 with the exception of centipede. (4.5-5.5). (The local
Cooperative Extension is a great help here.)
Applying fertilizers and humus to correct pH factor.
Raking the soil to clear rubble such as rocks, roots, weeds
tree roots, etc.
Tilling at least 6" deep, if possible
Watering deeply

Warm season grasses are best for Zone 8. They thrive in the
heat and become dormant when temperatures drop. Planting any
of these grasses is best done in early spring. There are four
grasses which fall into this category:

Bermuda grass - has a fine leaf, grows well in full sun and
requires fertilizing and watering often. It looks best when
mowed with a reel-type mower. Hybrids of bermuda grass
do best and may be sodded, seeded, plugged, sprigged, or
stolonized.

Zoysia (pronounced Zoy-see-ah) - is also a fine-leafed grass
and gives a high quality to a lawn. However, if planted in
full sun or very rich soil, it does not do as well. De-
thatching once a year will reduce lawn problems. It be a
very beautiful lawn grass - a lush green.

92

and is slow growing. Zoysia has to be sodded. It is purchased by the square yard and may be cut in small squares for planting. Though Zoysia is slow-growing, it is a rewarding grass once established because it needs mowing less frequently than the other grasses.

St. Augustine - has been the most popular grass across the South for years because of its growth in the shade. However, due to its susceptibility to SAD (a virus) and to chinch bugs, its popularity is decreasing. Newer varieties are being tested, and it may prove to be the hardiest of all the grasses still. To plant St. Augustine grass, the gardener may sprig, stolonize, or sod in squares bought from the local garden stores. St. Augustine cannot be planted by seeding. It is cold sensitive.

Centipede - is slow growing and needs less maintenance than the other grasses. Its leaf is of medium size and provides a beautiful lawn if watered faithfully. It can be seeded or sodded. It is fast becoming the most popular of available grasses with homeowners. It does not grow well under trees. Limit nitrogen - 1.5 lbs./1,000 sq. ft. yearly.

Rye Grass is quite popular in Zone 8 during winter months and early spring. Its leaf is very fine, and its apple green color provides a lovely foundation for spring bulbs, azaleas, and flowering trees, etc. This grass is planted only by seeding in early fall, one pound to 100 square feet. Watering deeply and frequently is recommended.

Once a lawn is established, maintenance consists of fertilizing, watering, and mowing. Feed in late winter or early spring with a balanced fertilizer (e.g. 8-8-8 or 13-13-13) following the manufacturer's directions. Fertilize again during the growing season to keep the lawn lush and colorful. Water well after each fertilizing.

CUTTING CHART

Bermuda	.5" - 1"	St. Augustine	1.5" - 3"
Zoysia	.5" - 1"	Centipede	1" - 2"

Raise mower blade 2 1/2 to 3 inches in hot summer days to prevent "scalping" your lawn.

Garden Care

Fertilizing the Landscape

All plants, like all people, require proper nutrition in order to remain healthy and disease free. In order to supply the proper nutrients for plants, one must first know the kind and amounts of nutrients that are available in the soil where the plants are to be grown.

No one can tell you what nutrients are available in a particular soil without first having a chemical analysis run on that soil. The accuracy of the analysis depends on the method used for collecting the soil sample.

A composite sample from each segment of the landscape to be treated will give an accurate indication of the plant nutrients that are in the soil. Using a hand trowel, soil auger, probe , or a shovel, take six to ten individual samples from random locations in the plot. Collect soil from the surface to a depth of four to six inches. Mix all of the samples together in a clean container and submit a pint of the mixture for analysis. This is called a composite sample.

Soil analysis is available through the Louisiana Cooperative Extension Service office in each parish in the state and here in the Monroe area at the Soil Testing Laboratory at Northeast Louisiana University. Both labs require some basic information such as the plants that are to be grown, the size of the plot, kinds and amounts of plant food (if any) that have been applied to the plot in the past few years, and the name and address of the person who submitted the sample. A basic soil analysis sheet will include the parts per million (PPM) of extractable phosphorus, extractable potassium, extractable calcium, extractable magnesium, the pH (acidity or alkalinity) of the soil, and the percent of organic matter that is present. Once this information is obtained, you will know what kind and how much of the major plant foods are necessary for optimum plant growth.

Nitrogen is also a major plant food. It promotes growth and is vital to all plant life. It isn't included in the basic soil analysis at the LSU Lab or at NLU. The reason is that the test for available nitrogen is difficult and not very reliable.

Phosphorus and potassium contribute to the health and vigor of plants, and both promote the development of strong, fibrous root systems.

Calcium and magnesium are also essential for the development of vigorous, healthy plants. When these two elements are available in the proper proportions at the proper ratio, plants are less likely to be diseased, and other plant foods such as phosphorus and potassium are more readily available to the plants.

In addition to fertilizer application, lawns and ornamentals also need suitable soil acidity for maximum growth. Most landscape plants like a slightly acid soil. As mentioned earlier in this writing, acidity and alkalinity in soils are expressed as soil pH on a scale from 0 to 14 - with a pH of 7 being neutral. Below 7 is acid; above 7 is alkaline. A pH of 6.0 to about 6.5 is usually about right for most landscape plants. Exceptions include azaleas and a few other landscape plants.

There are almost as many different soil types in this area of the state as there are plants that are used in the landscape, and each plant and each soil type requires a little different treatment. For this reason, it is of <u>utmost</u> importance that a soil analysis be obtained at about three-year intervals so that you can tell what kind and how much plant food you need for optimum plant growth.

In addition to the plant foods already discussed, there are additional elements sometimes referred to as micro-nutrients that are essential for plant growth. Sulfur, iron, zinc, boron, manganese, and molybdenum are some minor elements that are needed. Very few soils in our area are deficient in these nutrients. Some plants need these elements in greater amounts than others. For example, azaleas that are grown on soils with a pH of about 5.8 to above 6.0 can quickly become deficient in iron. A person trained in detecting these deficiencies can help with identifying micro-nutrient problems.

Remember, your Extension Service has bulletins on all types of landscape plants with the various plants' nutrition needs explained in detail. They can also help with lawn and garden maintenance recommendations.

Floyd Kent
Louisiana Cooperative
    Extension Service

Test Your Soil To Be Sure

The only way you can know what soil nutrients are needed is to have a soil analysis.

1. Take soil sample straight down 4" to 6" deep.

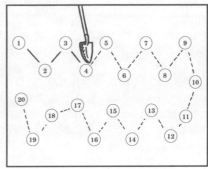

2. Take samples from each area in a zigzag pattern.

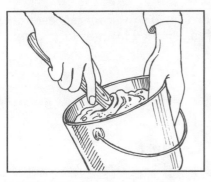

3. Mix samples from each section separately.

4. Take a pint of the mixed soil from each section. Label it accordingly. Take the pint from each section to the Extention Service Office in your parish.

5. Fill out the information sheet for each section. The sample and corresponding information will be sent to the soil lab. Analysis will be returned in 3-4 weeks.

Fertilizers

Organic fertilizers derive from animal and plant sources (e.g. manure, humus, etc.). They improve soil texture and provide a slow release of minerals.

Inorganic fertilizers are chemically produced balanced plant foods containing the three primary plant nutrients: nitrogen (N), phosphorus (P), and potassium (K). The percentage by weight of these elements is stated by numbers, always in the same sequence (e.g. 5-10-5, 8-8-8, etc.). Trace elements such as calcium, zinc, iron, etc. are sometimes added. There are fertilizers formulated specifically for acid-loving plants such as azaleas, camellias, and gardenias.

Commercial fertilizers may be purchased as granules, liquids, or water-soluble powders and are available in different strengths and formulations.

Follow directions on the product label to obtain the best and safest results. Plants can be injured or killed by over-fertilizing.

Plant Nutrients

NITROGEN - for above-ground growth, green foliage. Deficiency shown by slow growth and yellowing (chlorosis of leaves).

PHOSPHORUS - for healthy growth, strong root system, fruits and flowers. Deficiency shown by poor growth and dull reddish-purple leaves.

POTASSIUM - for general health, root formation, disease resistance. Deficiency shown by scorch around leaf edge which moves inward between veins.

Insects

Basically those insects that are present in Zone 8 fall into two main categories: harmful and beneficial. We all know that harmful insects must be controlled, but there are several insects that are of benefit to home gardens and landscapes. Without the dependable honeybee, proper pollination and viable seeds would be reduced or eliminated. In addition there are other beneficial insects that feed on harmful insects and are considered the natural enemy of several in the harmful category.

HARMFUL INSECTS

The harmful category can be divided into three basic groups: chewing, sucking, and scale insects. All of the above categories have to do with their feeding habits and, in a large degree, determine the method and materials used to control their populations. Notice the word "control", because in most instances eradication is nearly impossible.

Chewing Insects

In group one, there are those that chew the foliage, petals, bark, etc. of a plant. Included in this group are Japanese beetle, Spotted Cucumber beetle, Striped Cucumber beetle, Mexican Bean beetle, asparagus beetle, cabbage looper, imported cabbageworm, yellownecked caterpillar, Tent caterpillar, and grasshopper. Also included from time to time are crickets and leaf miners.

Sucking Insects

Group two is distinguishable as "sap-sucking" insects leaving the foliage but removing the chlorophyll and color. The feeding habits leave behind a curled, yellow, brown, wrinkled, or rolled appearance of foliage or flower parts. Sucking insects remove the very life blood of the plant.

Some of these insects are very small and often go undetected until the symptoms call for a closer inspection. Many of these sucking insects feed on the underside of the leaves so as to avoid the heat, rain, predators, and sprayed materials.

Those insects that feed through a siphoning, piercing mouthpart are these: leaf hopper, leaf bugs, aphids, mites, thrips, spittlebug, white flies, and the Southern stinkbug.

Scale Insects

Group three includes the scale insects. There are many genera of scale insects. The family Diaspididae is the largest family of scale insects, some of the most common being oyster shell, cottony cushion, woolly apple, and tortoise.

They can be seen clustering on twigs and branches of many plants. They appear lifeless during most of their lives. However, they do move, and it's during this time that they are most vulnerable. Both males and females have small flattened, oval bodies that are protected by a waxy scale covering. This covering is made from their own secretions and the cast off skins of their nymphal development stages. Males are usually more elongated but smaller than females. The adult females do not have eyes, legs, or antennae. The males have wings, legs, and antennae.

Reproduction is via both eggs and live birth. The young have short legs and use them to move about to feed. As they mature, they become stationary and attach themselves to their host by their mouthparts.

CONTROL OF INSECT PESTS

Control of the group one and group two insects consists of using one of the many reliable insecticides. Many of these are available in a dust form, but spraying and wetting the surface of the plant is more effective in controlling the insects.

The mites that are found on some ornamentals have to be controlled by using a miticide. These are very few in number and should be used only when a mite problem has been identified. Another treatment is the use of systemic granules. For more specific identification and treatment, visit with your local county agent.

Because of the nature of the scale insects, these small armor-covered pests are very difficult to control if not treated at the correct time of their life cycle. The object is to catch them with their "coats" off so as to wipe out a generation and break the reproductive cycle. Using insecticide in a normal manner does little to remove these pests. The most effective method of controlling scale insects is to use dormant oil or oil emulsion during cold weather to smother the scales by cutting off their supply of oxygen.

103

BENEFICIAL INSECTS

Often overlooked is the group of beneficial insects. This group of insects may be destroyed in our mad rush to eradicate harmful insects from that special bed or area of our landscape. Let's look at a few of these insects in this most productive and helpful category.

Pollinators

The first pollinators that come to mind in this category are the honeybees. They do an excellent job of pollinating almost every blooming plant in the landscape. The worker bee spends so much time working that its life expectancy is only 15-17 days!

Any insecticide that controls the harmful insects will also eliminate the honeybee. Therefore, the standard recommendation for insecticide application is to apply the product in the late afternoon. By this time of the day, most bees have done their day's work and are busy around the hive with cooling, cleaning, and feeding chores.

Other pollinators include the moths and butterflies and other members of the hymenoptera order. By the way, there are about 17,100 of these in North America, and most of them are found in Zone 8.

Predators

This group of insects feeds on the eggs, larvae, or adult insects that are harmful to men and plants.

The family Ichneumonidae is a very large family of parasitic wasps. The larvae stage of this family is parasitic of a wide variety of insects and spiders. Some of the adults lay their eggs in or on harmful insects, and these insects serve as hosts for the developing stages of the parasitic wasps.

The tiger beetle, often seen scampering along on barren soil in the warmest part of the day, is a beneficial insect that we often, in haste, try to crush with our size-whatever shoe heel.

The most famous of the beneficial beetles is the "lady beetle." Correctly, they are ladybug beetles and number in the hundreds in a given area during warmer weather. These can be ordered by mail, and they do a good job of lowering the number of aphids in the area.

To name some of the more common "ladybugs" in Zone 8, look

for the two-spotted, nine-spotted, the spotless, Ashy Gray, and the Convergent beetle.

Not to mention the Mantids (or walking sticks) would be leaving out one of the most misunderstood, but most common, predator insects. These insects are greatly elongated with almost cylindrical bodies. They have amazing ability to regenerate lost legs.

The Northern Walking Sticks and the Giant Walking Sticks are the most common. From time to time, one may see a Chinese Mantid, a Praying Mantis, Obscure Ground Mantid, or Carolina Mantid. Others include the Mantidfly and the Brown Mantidfly.

These insects feed on other insects. Included in their diet are ants, caterpillars, flies, butterflies, bees, and moths.

These pre-historic looking insects often frighten the home gardener into a reactionary destructive act. Leave 'em be! They are your friends and helpers.

Howard D. Gryder
County Agent
Ouachita Parish
Louisiana Cooperative
  Extension Service

Due to rapid changes in chemical control, we suggest calling your county agent for current information.

Diseases

Plant diseases can be divided into three main concerns for Zone 8 gardeners: fungal, bacterial, or viral. The first two can be controlled or corrected by treatment; control of the latter must come through clean seed selection or resistant varieties.

The most common problems we encounter are fungal. Many fungi are present all times of the year, especially during the wetter spring months and during early fall. When conditions are ideal for them to reproduce, their numbers are multiplied several times over by the erupting main bodies and the air-borne spores. When these spores land on healthy tissue, tiny root-like structures attach the spore to the plant's surface. At that point, the spore begins to feed on the plant sap. Soon a discolored spot or streak occurs, and when the chlorophyll is lost, so is the ability (of that portion of the plant) to make food.

As the spore feeds and reproduces, the amount of leaf tissue affected increases to a point that reduces the ability of the plant to bloom and fruit.

The application of fungicides protects the healthy tissue from the invading spores. It does not and will not restore tissue that has been affected.

As we consider the categories of plant diseases, it seems that one of the logical ways to look at this subject is to divide the plants into categories rather than the diseases. Let's consider the flowering plants, first.

FLOWERING PLANTS

The diseases that destroy or damage the plants in this category are bacterial leaf spot, blight, and stem rot; damping off; powdery mildew; grey mold; rust; anthracnose; and wilt. Does the list seem long? It really seems long when you begin to try to decide which is which! So many of the symptoms are similar.

To build an effective arsenal against these diseases, be sure to have on hand a variety of reliable insecticides, pesticides, and fungicides. Read the labels closely or talk to your local County Extension Agent about which to use for what problem. On some occasions, the garden center or store where you purchase the products can give valuable information. The use of these products

is very much like a doctor's prescription; if the directions say two tablespoons per gallon of water and apply every ten days, that's exactly what it means. Follow the directions!

GROUND COVERS AND VINES

These plants are somewhat widely varied in their ability to withstand abuse.

In this category, we are listing the Ajuga, English Ivy, Honeysuckle, Jasmine, Juniper, and Vinca as the most often used in landscapes in Zone 8.

The diseases that affect this group are not much different from the ones listed above; crown gall, leaf blight, leaf spot, root rot, dieback wither tip, dieback, and twig blight.

The use of a fixed copper is widely recommended for the treatment of many fungal-caused diseases, although there are other reliable fungicides on the market.

WOODY ORNAMENTALS

This group of plants has just what the name implies - woody stems. The diseases that are most often found in this group are a bit more involved and larger in number: root rot, leaf and twig blight, leaf spots and dieback, anthracnose, leaf gall, petal blight, chlorosis, nematodes, rust, fireblight, brown spot, bacterial stem rot, powdery mildew, needle blight, fusiform rust, canker, crown gall, sooty mold, leaf scorch, leaf blister, limb blight, scab, oak root rot, and leaf rust.

As you realize, there are many diseases that affect this group of plants. However, if one closely studies the plants he has in his landscape, he quickly recognizes the normal and abnormal plant characteristics. When the normal begins to look abnormal, treatment is needed. (Operate before the patient dies.)

The regular use of fungicide usually pays dividends. When the foliage of most of our ornamentals becomes damaged, the beauty of the plant begins to wane. If not treated, not only the foliage, but the bloom will be affected. Fungicides do the job for maintaining plant foliage in good health.

The use of products according to the label will result in controlling most of the diseases. There is no substitute for sanitation and good fertility practices.

LAWNS AND TURF

Basically there are four disease problems with lawns in Zone 8. These are Brown Patch, Dollar Spot, Slime Mold, and Melting Out. Some others that may occur on an occasional basis are SAD (St. Augustine Decline), rust, pythium blight, grey leaf spot, and nematodes (insects).

To control the main diseases, there is a variety of materials that can be used either as a spray or broadcast and watered in. During the time that lawn grasses are infected by fungi, fertilization should be discontinued. If watering is needed, apply it early enough in the day that the foliage will be dry before nightfall.

TREES

Large shade trees and nut trees will have to be treated by professionals who have the right equipment to reach the tops and provide complete coverage.

Should you have fruit trees in your landscape, contact your local county agent for specific spray schedules.

Howard D. Gryder
Ouachita Parish
Louisiana Cooperative
  Extension Service

Methods of Propagation

Propagation of plants is an interesting and inexpensive way of producing new plants from the parent stock. There are several methods of propagation; some are quite simple, while others challenge the gardener's skill and patience. All of these methods can be rewarding and fun provided one has the time and inclination:

1. Division
2. Simple Layering
3. Air-Layering
4. Grafting
5. Stolons
6. Seeds
7. Cuttings

DIVISION

Division is the simplest of the methods of propagation. It involves dividing a plant gently by the roots or by the crown into two or more smaller plants and potting each division. Any plant that sends up more that one stem through the surface of the soil can be divided this way. (e.g. ferns, violets, daylilies). Flowering plants should be divided when they are not in flower. Remember that the roots start drying out as soon as they are exposed, so re-pot as soon as possible. Water the new plants and place them in a bright spot out of direct sunlight; then, water sparingly until the new foliage is firm and healthy.

SIMPLE LAYERING

If a branch is low and sweeping and can be bent to the ground easily (e.g. azaleas, hydrangeas), scrape it on the underside, bury the scraped part about two inches, and place a brick or any heavy article on top. Never separate the selected branch from the parent plant until you see the new plant sprouting. Then you are certain that the operation has been successful. Layers are usually made in the spring, in order that roots may develop by fall.

AIR-LAYERING

Air-layering and grafting are possibly the more complicated methods of propagation. By using the air-layering method, you create a new plant or "clone" while retaining the original plant. Thus, you are the proud owner of two plants! This is a slow method but one that works, as it takes advantage of the circulatory system of the original plant. It is often used with plants that have grown too tall such as rubber trees, dracaenas, dieffenbachias.

Steps in the air-layering method:

1. Select a portion of the plant that will make a good short specimen.
2. Make an upward cut about 1/3 of the way through the stem at the spot where you want the roots to form.
3. Prop the cut open with a match or toothpick and dust the cut with a root stimulator (root hormone).
4. Take a wad of moistened sphagnum moss and tie it around the plant's stem, covering the cut.
5. Tie clear plastic around the moss to hold in the moisture. (After a few months you will see roots forming through the moss.)
6. Take the plastic wrapping off; cut off the stem just below the new roots.
7. Pot the new plant - roots, moss, and all. The old plant will now leaf out and become more shapely.

Air layering is usually most successful if done in the spring or late summer, as rooting is most vigorous in cool weather. Damp soil is most important for this procedure.

GRAFTING

The practice of grafting is tedious and slow in results. Moreover, it demands more skill and specialized knowledge than any other method of propagation. Like any activity, however, it becomes easier and more successful with practice. Don't be afraid to try. Grafting is used to unite the growing tissue of two botanically related plant varieties (e.g. sasanquas and camellias). Always graft on understock (stem or branch of a rooted plant) having a strong root system.

General steps for grafting:

1. Insert the base of the plant shoot, known as the "scion," into the previously made incision in the understock.
2. Bind the two tightly together. Good contact is essential.
3. Cover with a large jar or with grafting wax so that moisture is retained and the union is established.
4. Cut off any suckers that form below the point of union in order to give all possible strength to the new growth.

STOLONS

Stolons are underground suckers or trailing branches or runners which root when they come in contact with the soil. They can be severed from the parent plant and transplanted after roots have formed. These are characteristics of grasses, verbena and ajuga to name a few. The spider plant is also a good example.

110

SEEDS

Having collected seeds from the parent plant, you should recognize that a number of factors insure successful seed propagation: properly prepared soil; good, fresh seeds; the right amount of sun, shade, and moisture. If planting purchased seeds, note the expiration date on the packet. Plant the seeds thinly and press the soil firmly over them. Extremely fine seeds such as petunias should be mixed with sand.

Plants propagated by seeds sometimes have characteristics different from the parent. This is not generally known, but true, and also a disappointing factor at times.

Plants propagated by layers, grafts, or cuttings have characteristics exactly the same as the parent plant, and for this reason, many people prefer those means of propagation.

CUTTINGS

This is the simplest method of propagating plants, but by no means the surest. Cuttings may be made from stems or leaves of healthy plants using a clean, sharp knife.

Stem cuttings should be made from mature growth just below an eye or bud into lengths containing three or four eyes. Strip all the surplus leaves from the stem except the upper two. Never forget or underestimate the importance of using a good root stimulator. Place the cutting in 1 part sand and 1 part vermiculite. The roots develop from a callus formed on the cut surface. When roots are formed, there will be new top growth on the cutting. Transplant the plant in good garden soil when the roots are about one inch long.

> You may want to experiment with cuttings in a glass of water (e.g. aucuba, willow, impatiens).

Leaf cuttings are usually taken from plants that are fleshy or succulent. Place them immediately in damp soil and bright light. Mist the leaf often so the roots will sprout. Notable successes are gloxinias, African violets, and many begonias.

Cuttings of most plants root within two months. It is best to root them by fall. Those made in winter should be rooted by spring. Some cuttings take as long as a month to show roots, so do not despair!

111

Pruning Ornamentals

WHY PRUNE

1. To preserve natural character of plant while still reducing its size for a particular location
2. To increase flower size and quality
   Examples: Camellias and roses
3. For training purposes
   A. Espaliered plant
      1. Pyracantha
      2. Sasanqua
      3. Evergreen pear
      4. Loquat (Japanese Plum)
   B. Special Landscape Oddities
4. To remove dead, diseased, or weak wood
   A. After freezes
   B. Insect damaged wood
   C. Diseased portions
5. To reclaim overgrown shrubs
   Some shrubs such as ligustrum, holly, and others can very easily get out of hand in a short time. Two years without pruning may require severe pruning to reclaim a large, overgrown specimen.
6. To aid in transplanting
   Large volumes of roots are unavoidably cut off in the process of digging a shrub for transplanting. To compensate for this loss of roots, the above ground portions of the plant should be reduced proportionally. Completely remove some of the older branches. Prune others back to smaller side branches, remembering at <u>all</u> times to maintain the natural shape of the plant.

   If possible root prune one season before transplanting down into the roots at a point about two-thirds the distance from the crown to the spread of the branches. Some thinning of the top of the shrub should accompany this root-cutting treatment at transplanting.
7. To make harvesting, spraying, and cultivation easier
   Large overgrown plants such as camellias need to be pruned for proper spraying. Fruit trees need selective pruning to

make the tree grow into a particular form for ease of harvest and maintenance.

WHEN TO PRUNE

A. Spring flowering shrubs - after they bloom

B. Evergreens and summer flowering shrubs - winter

It is a good practice to cut small amounts from evergreen plants throughout the year. When more drastic pruning is necessary, prune in December, January, and February.

C. Storm damaged trees - saw off damaged limbs immediately after damage occurs. All cuts over 2 inches in diameter should be coated with a tree sealing compound.

HOW TO PRUNE

1. Remove fast growing suckers at the base of large plants that have trunks, such as crape myrtle.

2. Remove dead wood or diseased branches.

3. Remove large stems that cross.

4. Leave no stubs. Make cuts flush at a primary branch or trunk.

5. Prune plant according to its natural habit of growth. From within, thin out approximately one-third of the tallest canes. Cuts should be made at different heights. Where cuts are made, new growth will appear.

MATERIALS NEEDED

1. Hand shears

2. Long handled loppers

3. Pruning saw

4. Tree sealing compound

CAUTIONS

Unless you are a professional arborist, keep your feet on the ground! No ladders, no boxes, no buckets.

Dr. Neil Odenwald
Professor of Landscape Design
LSU   Baton Rouge, LA

REMOVING LARGE TREE LIMBS

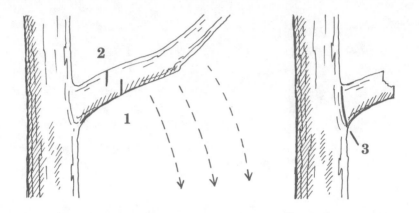

Make first cut from below at 1; cut off the limb from above at 2; then remove the stub with a cut at 3.

PRUNE BRANCHES TO SIDE BRANCHES

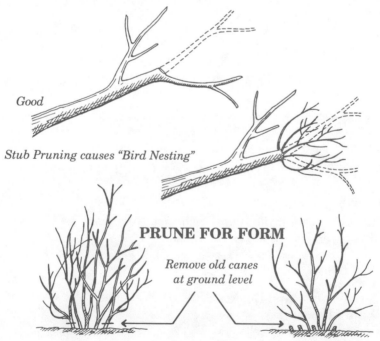

Good

Stub Pruning causes "Bird Nesting"

PRUNE FOR FORM

Remove old canes
at ground level

Rejuvenation To Induce New Compact Growth

Southern Favorites

Azaleas

The beauty of an azalea bed in full bloom is a glorious welcome to spring. Abundant lovely flowers in brilliant colors cover the entire plant, making a spectacular show.

Azaleas are classified in the genus Rhododendron. They can be evergreen or deciduous, from dwarfs to large shrubs. Flowers are basically tube-shaped single, double, or hose-in-hose (one flower inside the other). The colors range from white to soft or vivid shades of yellow, orange, pink, red, salmon, lavender, and purple. They are a highly successful and important shrub in Zone 8 as well as in colder and warmer zones as long as proper consideration is given to their cultural needs (i.e. soil, location, drainage, etc.).

In The Landscape

There are many possibilities for the use of evergreen azaleas because of their variety in size and color. Mature plant size and growth habits of different varieties should influence your selection for the garden. If they are used in foundation planting, consideration of your house color as a background is important. Mass planting of one color is effective in the landscape, especially if punctuated with white as a border or backing. Compatible evergreen shrubs provide a good background and serve as a pleasant contrast, particularly in foundation planting.

Mixed colors are also used in foundation planting and are widely used in naturalistic plantings, with white used to heighten and blend. Mixing colors takes careful planning to avoid a splotchy look.

Since bloom time is short, foliage should also be a selection factor. Choose compact, lush foliage particularly for closely viewed areas. Also, some azaleas give fall foliage color.

Planting

Azaleas are very shallow rooted and may be planted any time in the spring, fall, or mild winter. As with other shrubbery, fall planting is best to allow the plant to become established before cold winter and hot summer. Spring planting during bloom season allows for best color placement but demands special attention to watering and mulching during the hot summer.

Soil mix should be 5 parts garden soil (loam not clay), 4 parts peat moss or humus, 1 part builder's sand.

If a plant is container grown, remove the container. These plants are usually root-bound, so you must make several cuts from top to bottom of the ball where the ball touched the container, to free the root system to grow into the soil. If you purchase burlap wrapped plants, carefully cut away the top half of the burlap.

Dig a hole 2 to 3 times the size of the ball (you may use the top 4 to 6 inches of soil in your soil mix and discard the rest); then add your soil mix so that the ball will be 2 to 3 inches above the surrounding level to compensate for settling. Bring the soil halfway up on the ball, water, and then fill the hole, lightly tamping the soil close to the ball. Mulch with pine straw, pine bark chips, or other organic material and water well. Remember not to plant too deeply nor smother with excessive mulch.

Cut cans with tin shears or notched screwdriver. Make two cuts, on opposite sides. Be careful of sharp edges.

Roots that encircle the root ball must be pulled loose. Use your fingers, or a knife to loosen them, but don't break the soil ball.

Growth Requirements

Partial shade is best for most azaleas. Dense shade inhibits growth and bloom. Some varieties can tolerate full sun.

Good drainage is essential. Azaleas should be moist, but water should not stand in the bed.

Azaleas prefer acid soil with a pH factor (degree of acidity) of 5.0 to 6.0. Proper pH balance makes proper nutrients available to the plants. Have your soil tested before the bed is prepared and follow corrective recommendations.

Maintenance

Fertilizing. Special azalea fertilizer is available with instructions for proper application. If you prefer you may use a balanced fertilizer (e.g. 8-8-8) at a recommended rate of 1/2 cup per square yard of bed, or cottonseed meal at the rate of 1/4 lb. per square yard of bed. Plants should be fertilized after blooming and may be fertilized again in 6 to 8 weeks. Too much fertilizer can damage or kill plants. Always water thoroughly after application.

Watering. A good soaking once a week should be sufficient. In times of extreme heat or drought and when buds are developing (late summer - early fall), more watering is necessary. A good soaking prior to freezing weather gives the plant extra protection.

Pruning. Prune azaleas for cut flowers while in fresh bloom. Prune out dead wood or long leggy growth after bloom. If older plants have become overgrown, it is best to prune them back over a period of several years rather than shock the plant with severe cut-back.

Problems

Yellowing Leaves. Yellowing leaves showing green veins indicate iron deficiency. Chelated iron can be sprayed on plants and ground surface for temporary correction. For a long-term solution, acidify the soil by adding iron sulfate or aluminum sulfate. If leaves are spotted or brown on the edges, magnesium is needed. Sprinkle Epsom salts around the plant.

*Petal Blight (*Fungus). Flowers look totally wilted as though hot water has been poured over them. Plants and soil must be sprayed with protective material every 2 to 3 days while in flower and again just before flowering the following spring. Follow the manufacturer's directions for application of the proper fungicide.

Leaf Gall. Thickened, curly leaves which lose their color and then turn brown indicate this problem. Pick and destroy these leaves if possible or spray with fungicide.

Pests. An oil-base spray after bloom is recommended for protection against most pests, especially scale. Others, such as thrips, lacebugs, and spider mites can be controlled with insecticide sprays according to the manufacturer's directions.

Propagation

Cuttings and layering are the easiest methods. Cuttings should be taken in late spring when new growth has matured

some. You can make a cutting bed or box, but more simply just push cuttings into the soil in the azalea bed. Keep the soil moist until the cuttings are rooted; then transplant. To layer, make a V-shaped cut, or scrape the bark where a low branch touches the ground; cover with soil and mulch, and weight with a stone. Check for roots in the fall and transplant.

Varieties

The following list of varieties is taken from information provided to the public by the Cooperative Extension Service of Louisiana State University and Agricultural and Mechanical College in cooperation with the United States Department of Agriculture. There are, of course, many more varieties which could be considered. If you have seen a variety which appeals to you, try it in your garden and perhaps it will do well for you with your "Tender Loving Care."

Evergreen Azaleas

Indian or Indica - Fast growing large plants (some 8 to 10 feet); large flowers bloom early to mid-season.

White
Fielder's White	King's White	New White
Indica Alba	Mrs. G. G. Gerbing	

Orange-Red
Duc de Rohan	William Bull	Prince of Orange
President Clay		

Red
Charles Encke	Dixie Beauty	Pride of Dorking

Pink
Fisher Pink	Prince of Wales	Southern Charm
Pride of Mobile	Elegans	

Salmon
Daphne Salmon	Glory of Sunnyhill	Judge Soloman
Duke of Wellington		

Purple/Lavender
Formosa	George Taber	Gulf Pride

Kurume and other Japanese Types - Hardy, more compact plants 4 to 6 feet high with smaller leaves than Indian variety; good bloomers in a wide color range.

White

Glacier	H. H. Hume	Snow

Orange-Red

Copperman	Fashion

Red

Christmas Cheer	Hexe	Hinodegiri
Flame		

Pink

Coral Bells	Pinocchio

Salmon

Bridesmaid	Sweetheart Supreme	Salmon Beauty
Pink Pearl		

Satsuki Hybrids - Very low mounded growth habit (height 12 - l5 inches) with small dark green leaves. Large flowers bloom in May and June. The following selection of recommended plants of the Satsuki variety is taken from Identification Selection and Use of Southern Plants for Landscape Design by Dr. Neil G. Odenwald and Mr. James R. Turner:

White

White Gumpo	Bunka *(white with*	Myogi *(white with*
Gunbi *(white with*	*red edges)*	*pink streaks)*
red flecks)		

Pink

Pink Gumpo	Gunrei	Pink Macrantha

Red

Red Gumpo	Red Macrantha

Deciduous Azaleas

The native deciduous azaleas are more suited to naturalistic planting as their growth pattern is tall and leggy. If used in a traditional bed, a good background is necessary. They bloom in early spring and are usually very fragrant. These plants will

sometimes tolerate poorly drained or even swampy areas. Consult a local expert concerning planting, maintenance, etc.

Native

White to Pink

Honeysuckle *(blooms before foliage)*

Texas *(blooms late May-June)*

Creamy White

Swamp, Summer or Hammocksweet *(blooms July-August)*

Introduced Species

Yellow, Orange to Orange-Red

Florida   Japanese   Chinese

(All three bloom before foliage)

Caution: Azaleas are shallow-rooted. Don't work around them. Protect them with mulch.

Camellias

There is considerable variation in individual preference regarding camellia varieties. One of the best ways to get an idea of choices available is to attend a well planned camellia show. It is important to get good plants in your choice of varieties. Selections consist of those plants that bloom very early to those that bloom very late, with some blooming midseason.

Varieties that Bloom Very Early

Daikagura (var) *(red/white)*   High Hat *(pink)*

September Morn *(white)*   Arejishi *(red)*

Varieties that Bloom Early to Midseason

Mathotiana *(purple dawn)*   Debutante *(pink)*

Alba Plena *(white)*   Doris Ellis *(white/pink)*

White Empress   Empress *(rose)*

Gregory Conway *(white)*   Ville de Nantes *(variegated

Prof. Sargent *(red double)*   red)*

Pink Perfection

Varieties that Bloom Midseason to Late

Thelma Dale *(rose)*   Elegans *(pink)*

Glen 40 *(red)*   Victory *(white)*

Charlotte Bradford *(rose)*

Varieties that Bloom Late

Pink Champagne   Blood of China *(red)*

Location

Since location largely determines whether camellias may be successfully grown, good drainage should be the first consideration in making your decision. Unless the soil is well-drained, the growth of the camellia will not be satisfactory. Many excellent specimens die annually because they are planted in poorly drained soil.

Although partial shade is essential for growth of small camellia plants, some shade is also beneficial to larger ones. Pine trees provide excellent shade for camellias.

Planting

It is true that camellias can be transplanted at any time of the year if they are handled properly and a sufficient ball of soil remains on the root system. The ideal time, however, is in November or early December. Expect an 85-90% survival rate of plants purchased in containers; bare-rooted plants have about a 75% survival rate.

If possible, it is best to select a location several months in advance of the time of planting. The hole should be dug and some decayed organic matter worked into the soil as the hole is refilled. No commercial fertilizer should be added at this time, with the possible exception of a small amount of superphosphate when the hole is prepared.

It is <u>very important</u> not to set the plants too deep. Never plant them deeper than they were in the nursery row. If the plant is set too deep, and is unhealthy, it may sometimes benefit by being raised or by being moved to a more favorable location.

Under good conditions, camellia plants should live over 50 years; however, they must be given a space of about 6 feet in which to grow.

Soils

Camellia plants are grown in a wide range of soils, but they do not adapt well to very heavy soils. In any case, a high percentage of organic matter should be present. This may be supplied in the form of leaf or woods mold, or well decomposed manure to which no lime or other chemicals have been added. Cow manure is preferable to other kinds of manure. Peat moss is often used as a source of organic matter. A mixture of one part organic matter (peat, well-rotted manure, leaf mold, etc.), one part top soil, and one part sand is satisfactory for camellias. An acid soil with a pH of 5 to 5.5 should be sufficient.

Fertilizing

In general, an 8-8-8 fertilizer applied at the rate of 1/8 to 1/4 pound per plant is recommended. Uniformly scatter it over the soil area covered by the spread of the plant. Fertilize in late winter or early spring in advance of the first growth period so the fertilizer can be utilized at that time. One fertilization per year is adequate except on very poor soil.

Watering

Although good drainage is essential for the well being of camellia plants, sufficient water to meet their requirements is also necessary. It is especially important that they do not suffer from lack of water for the first two years after being transplanted. The second year is especially important, for that is when they are most likely to be neglected. In watering the plants, the ground should be thoroughly soaked, then not watered again for about a week.

Mulching

A mulch of pine needles, pine bark, hay, well-rotted sawdust, etc. is beneficial to camellias until they are large enough to make their own shade. Mulch serves several useful purposes: it conserves moisture, keeps the surface cooler, helps to keep weeds and grasses from growing, adds organic matter to the soil, and reduces danger from cold injury to the crown of the plant. It is recommended that the mulch be from two to three inches deep.

Pruning

Plants can be kept from getting too large by pruning, which should be done after the blooming period is over and before growth starts anew. Large wounds should be covered with a good protective material. It is suggested that pruning be started when plants are small, thus making drastic pruning unnecessary.

It is recommended that plants with a dense growth be thinned to allow for more efficient spraying. The deeply shaded limbs and twigs produce few good flowers; moreover, they do harbor scales, and the density of the branches makes it very difficult for the spray material to be effective.

Buds

If specimen flowers are desired, bloom buds should be reduced to one per shoot. Pinch off any side buds.

Use of Gibberellic Acid

When using gibberellic acid, a growth promoting acid, varieties bloom earlier, and very often flowers become larger. Getting earlier blooms is important in that many varieties can be forced to bloom before severe freezes, as well as allowing them to bloom ahead of petal blight in areas where this disease is found. Refer to the segment on petal blight below.

Gibbing camellia flower buds. Select well-developed flower bud, remove vegetative bud, and place one drop of acid in the cup left where vegetative bud was removed.

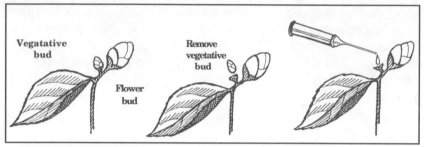

Louisiana Cooperative Extension Service

Cutting Blooms

When plants are very small, few, if any, blooms should be cut. The blooms may be twisted off without injury to the terminal growth bud if done carefully. Such blooms are good for floating in shallow containers. When plants attain moderate size, cutting the blooms is not harmful. Having flowers to share with friends or have in the home, to wear as corsages, or to enter in flower shows is a large part of the pleasure of growing camellias.

Propagation

Camellias may be propagated by seed, cuttings, layering and air layering, or grafting.

PROBLEMS AND TREATMENTS

Petal Blight

With petal blight, brownish specks appear and enlarge as the flowers expand. Every effort should be made to prevent the spread of this very serious disease.

The best method is to pick up all the fallen blooms and petals and safely discard them.

Scale

Because of scale insects, camellias should be sprayed at least once a year in the spring with an oil spray. Spray the underside of every leaf.

Annie Mae Hathorn
Camellia Judge

Daffodils

Daffodils are certainly one of the easiest of all flowers to grow. They are one of the best for cut flowers, and they come at a most welcome time. By planting early and late varieties (cultivars), you can expect blooms for more than two months. More than fifty bulbs can be planted in the space required for one rose bush. If the proper varieties are planted, they should outlast our grandchildren.

Not all types or varieties of daffodils do well in Zone 8, but many do. They come in many forms and colors, more than most people have seen.

Here are a few simple requirements for planting and caring for daffodils:

Plant varieties known to do well in our area unless you want to have fun experimenting.

Choose a well-drained location with half to full sun. Sometimes, nature provides too much water during summer unless drainage is good. Plant daffodils out of range of summer sprinklers unless you don't mind the task of digging, storing, and replanting each year. The deeper the topsoil, the better; but use no manure, fresh compost, or bark as these encourage basal rot. Sphagnum peat, vermiculite, perlite, and coarse sand are fine, but expensive.

The middle of October is an ideal time to plant daffodils in our area. Dig soil at least a spade deep. Plant bulbs 6 to 8" apart and 4 to 6" deep, depending on bulb size. Do not mix fertilizer in the soil, but spread it on top after planting. Use low nitrogen fertilizer such as 5-10-10. Fertilize established bulbs each October. Spread 2 lbs. per 10' x 10' on top of the soil as you did after planting. Do not use bone meal as this can encourage rot and cause pests to root. Half this amount of fertilizer can be repeated in mid-January on yellow types, but avoid over-fertilizing whites and more delicate types as this can encourage rot.

After the bulbs have matured and the foliage has yellowed, they should not be watered. Do not cut or mow foliage until it has turned yellow.

Winter vegetation will compete with daffodils, but summer weeds do not. However, summer vegetation is unsightly and can become hard to remove. Some people use mulch

such as pine straw. This helps control weed growth and will keep the flowers cleaner while blooming. However, this mulch can encourage the slugs and may retain too much moisture on the bulbs.

Daffodils will need dividing every 3 to 5 years. Early June is the ideal time, and bulbs can be re-planted at this time. Do not plant bulbs during July and August heat.

To dry bulbs, take them to the shade as soon as they are dug, wash them with a hose, but do not brush. Spread them out and store them in a cool, dry, well-ventilated place. Turn them every week for the first month and discard any rotted ones. Rats will not eat daffodil bulbs.

Yellows, as a rule, bloom earlier than more colorful ones. Also, they are generally more resistant to basal rot, our only major problem. Whites and a few more delicate ones are more subject to rot. Basal rot kills the bulbs. They can be chemically treated, but the best bet is to choose more resistant varieties.

Most daffodil bulbs are grown in England, not Holland as most people believe. These bulbs, along with many from our East and West Coasts, are intercepted by the Dutch dealers and sold to us as "Dutch" bulbs. The "Dutch" market, through local dealers and numerous catalogs, offers us very little choice, and many of these varities are not adapted to our zone.

Your local chapter of the American Daffodil Society is a reliable source of additional information including suppliers of quality bulbs.

D. Q. Rankin
Daffodill Grower

Hydrangeas

The hydrangea is a true international deciduous plant. It is native to North America and Eastern Asia and was introduced into England in 1790 by Joseph Banks. It has been developed by French and German patience into many distinct varieties. It has been so at home in the South that it is frequently called the "Southern Hydrangea." When in bloom, it is among the most glorious of plants.

The reasons for the hydrangeas' popularity, besides their beauty, are that they grow in shade and flower from spring to late summer. They are especially effective when massed in partial shade or when planted in large containers. Shelter from long exposure to the sun is necessary. They thrive and bloom under trees and along the north and east walls of houses. Plants along the east wall are usually deeper in color.

They are easy to grow in rich, porous soil and, being very shallow rooted, should be given shallow cultivation. From the time growth starts in the spring, the plants should receive water twice a week until the first buds form, and daily afterwards.

Soil should be on the acid side. Any loose soil containing nutriments is satisfactory. Oak leaves, decayed pine straw, or peat moss may be used to make it porous.

The plants respond well to fertilizer. Manure may be applied in winter, and other fertilizer may be used about the time the buds begin to form.

Rooting is easy. Cuttings may be made from either old or new wood, but there is less loss with new wood. A cutting may be made with one or two pairs of buds. The stem should be placed in porous soil with one pair of buds underground and the soil pressed firmly around it. Shade and constant moisture are essential. By fall the cuttings will have developed good roots and should be protected through the winter.

There are about 25 or more varieties of hydrangeas. An old garden favorite, the French or Big Leaf Hydrangea (*H. Macrophylla*), is a sturdy deciduous shrub that blooms in late spring and provides weeks of garden color. The most striking feature of the plant is the variation in flower color, which may vary from deep pink to white to deep blue, depending on soil pH. An abundance of lime makes the flowers pink. Too much lime will check the growth of the plants and cause a yellowing. Soil acidity may be

strengthened by the use of alum, rusty iron filings, or aluminum sulfate to make the blossoms blue. Consult your County Agent for the proper amount for your garden. Treatment to change the flower color should be started a year in advance.

The plant looks best when maintained at a height of four to six feet. This requires careful pruning immediately after flowering since the plant flowers on new growth. Cut back woody stems to a point just above a leaf bud where next year's growth will begin. Don't cut back unflowered shoots unless an overall thinning is desired.

The first hydrangea to bloom in the spring is the Oak-Leaf *(Hydrangea quercifolia)*, a native to the Southeastern United States. It has leaves shaped like the red oak and flowers which grow erect in cone-shaped spikes atop the foliage. The blossoms change from white to rose as they mature. Two superior selections are Snowflake and Harmony. This variety blooms on the current year's growth. Prune them, if necessary, after blooming.

Another Southern native is the Smooth Hydrangea *(H. arborescens)*, an upright grower with grayish green leaves and white sterile flowers in large roundish clusters which bloom from early summer to fall. Annabelle is the name of the most improved version. These plants bloom on new wood, so prune them back about one-third in late winter.

The Peegee *(H. paniculata grandiflora)* may grow to ten feet or more in height. In midsummer, white flowers in foot-long panicles appear, which slowly fade to pink. The abundance of heavy blossoms causes the branches to bend, creating a fountain of flowers. The winter effect on these blooms is striking, with the bronze color of the dry flowers adding an ornamental quality to the leafless plants. If pruning is necessary, cut back in early spring since the blooms come on the current year's growth.

Not too well known is the lace-cap form of French Hydrangea. Its beauty is subtle. The blossoms consist of tiny flowers ringed by large single flowerettes ranging in color from mauve-pink to white to blue, depending on soil acidity.

One final hydrangea is notable, the Climbing Hydrangea. One of the hardiest Southern woody vines, it clings by means of tiny aerial roots, climbs over 50 feet or as high as its support, but grows slowly so it seldom needs pruning. In May and June, expect beautiful white flowers on your vine.

Native Plants
Wildflowers Suggested for Cultivation
in Louisiana

Almost 2,000 species of native vascular plants occur in Louisiana. Many of these species could be easily cultivated in flower beds, lawns, and gardens. Some are aggressive enough to be planted along our roadsides. Wildflowers should be started from seeds or bought from nurseries that propagate their own plants. Only plants that will be destroyed by development, highway construction, clear-cutting, etc. should be "rescued" from death by being transplanted to our gardens. Some of the lesser known but showy wildflowers will be discussed below.

Spider lily *(Hymenocallis liriosome)* and swamp lily *(Crinum americanum)* are two members of the Amaryllis Family that have large showy white flowers. They are easily propagated from bulbs or from their fleshy seeds. These perennials will last a lifetime in a flower bed.

Jack-in-the-pulpit *(Arisaema triphyllum)*, green dragon *(Arisaema dracontium)*, and arrow arum *(Peltandra virginica)* are showy members of the Arum Family. They can be cultivated easily from seed or from corms. The arrow arum has dark green caladium-like leaves.

The Pickerel Weed Family contains two showy blue-flowered species. Water hyacinth *(Eichhornia crassipes)*, although a pest in bayous, is unsurpassed for its orchid-like flowers and can be easily grown in small pools and ponds. Pickerel weed *(Pontederia cordata)* produces large spikes of small dark-blue flowers. Each of these must be started from the abundant off-shoots.

Louisiana has 43 different species of orchids. All the large showy ones are rare and are almost impossible to cultivate because of their special habitat requirements including mycorrhizal fungi in their roots. Only the lady tresses *(Spiranthes, 12 species)* are common enough to cultivate. *Spiranthes odorata* produces large twisted spikes of white flowers with a strong odor that resembles that of tube-roses.

One of our most neglected groups of showy plants is the Milkweed Family. Several species of milkweeds can be cultivated from seeds or from root cuttings. The best known is a bright orange one known as chigger weed, butterfly weed, or pleurisy

root *(Asclepias tuberosa)*. Perhaps the easiest one to cultivate is the common shore or swamp milkweed *(A. perennis)* which has small white and pink flowers, and if the old flowers are removed, this plant will continue flowering until frost. All species are perennials but die back to the ground and overwinter as thick underground roots and rhizomes. Several other species have flowers from green to white to white mottled with purple.

Our largest group of flowers is in the Sunflower Family. These composites include many species of native and naturalized plants that are showy and easily cultivated. They can be grown from seeds or from off-shoots of perennial ones. These include asters *(Aster* - blue, purple, white, and blue and yellow flowers); Spanish needles *(Bidens* - bright yellow flowers); doll's daisy *(Boltonia* - white and yellow flowers); Indian plantain *(Cacalia* - white flowers); golden asters *(Heterotheca* - yellow flowers); tickseeds *(Coreopsis* - yellow or yellow and maroon flowers); purple coneflowers *(Echinacea* - purple flowers); fleabanes *(Erigeron* - white and pink flowers); bonesets and mist flowers *(Eupatorium* - white, pink, or blue flowers); Indian blanket *(Gaillardia* - yellow or red and yellow flowers); sunflowers *(Helianthus* - bright yellow flowers of several sizes); blazing stars *(Liatris* - purple to deep pink flowers); coneflowers *(Ratibida* - all lemon yellow or yellow and brown or bronze flowers); brown-eyed Susans *(Rudbeckia* - yellow and brown flowers); ragworts *(Senecio* - bright yellow flowers); and Stokes' aster *(Stokesia* - showy white and blue to pink flowers). Several other genera, both native and naturalized, are worthy of cultivation. Remember that all species of goldenrods *(Solidago)* make showy yellow displays in fall and late fall. Ragweeds *(Ambrosia)* and sumpweeds *(Iva)* are green-flowered and produce pollen that causes hayfever; goldenrods have never caused hayfever and should be used more extensively in home plantings.

The mayapple *(Podophyllum peltatum)* in the Barberry Family produces large, showy, umbrella-shaped leaves and spreads rapidly from underground rhizomes. It produces a flower about two inches across and edible fruits. The leaves are especially showy in a wooded area where they will form extensive populations, and their large white flowers are very fragrant.

The Bellwort Family contains the campanulas and the lobelias. Bellwort *(Campanula americana)* produces masses of bright blue flowers. It is an endangered plant in Louisiana, but its seeds are readily available from most seed companies. Lobelias vary from pale blue *(Lobelia appendiculata)* to dark blue *(L. puberula*

and *L. siphilitica)* to bright red *(L. cardinalis)*. The last species, cardinal-flower, is probably our most desirable wildflower for home cultivation. Its favorite habitat is a wet roadside ditch, but because of the spraying of herbicides by our parish and state road crews, over 90% of our native populations have disappeared. This plant is easily cultivated from seeds and spreads in flower beds. It should be extensively used to attract hummingbirds and just because of its innate beauty.

The Bean Family contains many genera of showy wild flowers. Most of these are easily grown from seeds. Milkvetches *(Astragalus)* produce clusters of cream to pink flowers. False indigos *(Baptisia)* produce large clusters of bright yellow to cream to white flowers. Butterfly pea *(Clitoria)* and butterfly pea vine *(Centrosema)* produce large showy blue flowers. Coral bean or mamou *(Erythrina herbacea)* produces large spikes of two-inch long red flowers sought by hummingbirds. The seeds are bright red and are used in rosary beads. Catgut or hoary pea *(Tephrosia)* produces flowers with pink and cream-colored petals in the same flower.

The members of the Mint Family are common and easily grown from seeds and from young off-shoots. Horsemints *(Monarda)* have flowers that are pink or purple or yellow with purple dots. Obedient plants *(Physostegia)* produce large showy clusters of pinkish-purple flowers. Mountain mints *(Pycnanthemum)* produce very fragrant foliage and clusters of white to purple flowers. Blue sage *(Salvia azurea)* has dark blue or snowy white flowers, and scarlet sage *(S. Coccinea)* has deep red flowers. Several species of skullcaps *(Scutellaria)* produce showy blue flowers.

Indian pink in the Logania Family is one of our easiest showy wildflowers to cultivate. *Spigelia marilandica* forms clumps of plants about 1.5 feet tall, and it produces masses of two-inch long flowers that are red on the outside and yellow on the inside. Yellow jasmine *(Gelsemium sempervirens)* is a favored yellow-flowered woody vine in this family.

The Mallow Family is noted for its large showy flowers. The poppy mallows or winecups *(Callirhoe)* produce showy wine-cup shaped flowers with varying shades of purple. Two species of hibiscus or wild cotton *(Hibiscus lasiocarpus* and *H. laevis)* produce white flowers up to 6 inches in diameter while another species *(Hibiscus aculeatus)* has smaller yellow flowers. Most species have inner purple throats. The marsh mallow *(Kosteletzkya)* has very showy pale-pink flowers. All these species are

perennial and produce clumps of plants up to six feet tall. They will flower longer if fruit is not allowed to develop. They are easily cultivated from their large okra-like seeds.

The Evening Primrose Family contains several showy plants. Gaura *(Gaura)* produces large spikes of pink showy plants. Seedboxes and water primroses *(Ludwigia)* produce yellow flowers worthy of cultivation. Primroses *(Oenothera)* produce very showy white, pink, or yellow flowers. All members of this family are best started from seeds.

The Phlox Family is well-known for its showy flowers. Our perennial native phlox *(Phlox divaricata, P. caroliniana,* and *P. pilosa)* are blue to purple and quite showy. They can be cultivated from seeds or from bought plants or those rescued from habitat destruction in nature. Annual phlox *(P. drummondii)* is a small annual with large nickel-sized flowers that vary from red to pink to white. It is easily grown from seeds that are readily available commercially.

The Figwort or Snapdragon Family has many showy species. The false foxgloves produce pink *(Agalinis)* or yellow *(Aureolaria)* foxglove-shaped flowers. Indian paintbrush *(Castilleja)* produces bright red flowers (bracts). Monkey flowers *(Mimulus)* produce pink to purple flowers. The beard-tongues *(Penstemon)* are easily-grown perennials that produce showy white or pink tubular flowers. The very rare *Penstemon murrayanus* produces red flowers. All of the members of this family are easily grown from seeds.

Many members of the Verbena Family have showy flowers. Lantana *(Lantana)* has flowers that are pink or orange or multicolored. Five species of verbena *(V. bipinnatifida, V. canadensis, V. rigida, V. tenuisecta,* and *V. xutha)* produce showy purple flowers. Moss vervain *(V. tenuisecta)* is a rapidly-spreading prostrate plant very desirable for mown roadsides and lawn margins. All can be grown from cuttings or from seeds.

Numerous other species of showy Louisiana native wildflowers can be successfully used in home plantings and in landscaping.

Woody Vines Available for Landscaping in Louisiana

There are several showy native woody vines in Louisiana that are suitable for almost any purpose for which vines are used in landscaping. Most of these are not too aggressive and have few natural enemies or pests.

Coral honeysuckle *(Lonicera sempervirens)* produces large numbers of red flowers that attract hummingbirds. This species is not aggressive like its Japanese relative *(L. japonica)*.

Yellow jasmine *(Gelsemm sempervirens)* is our most showy native vine and is widely used in landscaping. It is readily available from most clear-cut pine woods in the state.

Trumpet creeper *(Campsis radicans)* is too aggressive for most uses but produces showy flowers in areas where it can be controlled. It can be pruned to form a tree-form like wisteria. Some people are allergic to the leaves of this plant, hence the common name cow itch. Its close relative, cross vine *(Bignonia capreolata)*, is less aggressive and produces orange and yellow bi-colored flowers.

Coral berry or carolina snailseed *(Cocculus carolinus)* is worthy of cultivation for the red fruits in late fall.

Vine hydrangea *(Decumaria barbara)* does well in wet, sandy areas. Star-vine *(Schisandra glabra)* is a magnolia relative that produces pretty red flowers. It will grow in shaded areas.

Several native *Clematis* species are available for cultivation. The rare *C. glauca* produces showy pink flowers. *C. crispa* produces blue flowers. *C. reticulata* can be used only on sandy sites and produces numerous purple flowers that are usually called leather-flower. *C. virginiana*, virgin's bower, produces showy clusters of white flowers. The naturalized *C. ternifolia* produces showy displays of white flowers but is very aggressive.

The grape vine family *(Vitaceae)* contains several native and naturalized vines. The pepper vines *(Ampelopsis arborea* and *A. cordata)* are very aggressive but produce fruits that attract birds. The fruits on *A. arborea* turn from green to red and then black and are showy. The young vegetation has a pleasant red appearance. Post oak grape *(Vitis lincecumii)* produces large edible grapes and is worthy of cultivation in dry sandy areas. Muscadines or scuppernongs *(Vitis rotundifolia)* make showy vines on arbors and produce edible fruits but are inferior to cultivated forms. Virginia creeper *(Parthenocissus quinquefolia)* produces showy displays of red leaves (with 5 leaflets) in the fall. Its fruits are used by several kinds of birds.

Most species of greenbriers are pests. However, some people might desire to use some of them in landscaping. *Smilax walteri* has good-looking leaves and few thorns on the stems. Its red-berries in the fall make it an attractive vine. Sarsaparilla vine *(S.*

pumila) has no thorns. This evergreen vine makes a good ground cover, and it has attractive red berries in the spring. Its leaves can be used to make a tea good for the stomach ache. The two bamboo vines *(S. smallii and S. laurifolia)* are evergreen and would offer year-round greenery. Their young stems in the spring can be used for asparagus.

Our native wisteria (*Wisteria macrostachya*, Kentucky wisteria) can be used in any way the Chinese ones are except that it is not as aggressive.

Native plants usually fit the environment better than introduced "foreigners" and tend to "fit-in" rather than to "take-over" as do such things as Japanese honeysuckle and kudzu.

Louisiana Shrubs Available for Use in Landscaping

Several of our native shrubs are well-adapted to being used for plantings in lawns, parks, and along streets. The following group of plants includes plants that range from low shrubs to those that mature to sub-canopy size. Some are preferred for their evergreen leaves while others are chosen for their showy flowers or fruits. Check out special requirements of these in other books or consult a specialist. Scientific names are used to allow one to be sure which plant is being discussed. These shrubs are listed alphabetically by their family names.

ANACARDIACEAE - Cashew family
Aromatic sumac *(Rhus aromatica)* - small shrub with showy leaves.
Winged sumac *(Rhus copallina)* - red leaves in fall; red fruit.
Smooth sumac *(Rhus glabra)* - red leaves in fall; red fruit.
All three species tend to form thickets by root sprouts.

ANNONACEAE - Custard Apple Family
Pawpaw *(Asimina triloba)* - large magnolia-like leaves and edible fruits.
Dwarf pawpaw *(Asimina parviflora)* - small shrub with showy leaves and flowers.

AQUIFOLIACEAE - Holly Family
Our evergreen hollies include *Ilex cassine, I. coriacea, I. glabra, I. myrtifolia, I. opaca,* and *I. vomitoria.* Our other species are deciduous - *I. ambigua, I. amelanchier, I. decidua, I. laevigata, I. longipes, I. montana,* and *I. verticillata.*

All hollies vary in fruit color and leaf shape. All species are unisexual, so only half of the native plants produce fruit. Choose a plant with the desired leaves and fruits and propagate it by cuttings using rooting hormones and a mist bed.

ARALIACEAE - Aralia or Ginseng Family
Devil's -walkingstick *(Aralia spinosa)* - easily grown, large compound leaves and showy flowers followed by purple fruits that are choice food of songbirds.

ARECACEAE - Palm Family
Palmetto *(Sabal minor)* - slow-growing but easily grown from seed.

CALYCANTHACEAE - Calycanthus Family
Sweetshrub or bubby bush *(Calycanthus floridus)* - showy leaves and flowers. Pleasant odor of flowers makes a nice planting near windows.

BETULACEAE - Birch Family
Hazelnut *(Corylus americana)* - desirable for fruits and its clump-forming shape.
River birch *(Betula nigra)*, Muscle wood *(Carpinus caroliniana)*, and hop hornbeam *(Ostrya virginiana)* are large sub-canopy plants but make well-shaped plants when planted in lawns. Alders *(Alnus serrulata)* do well in wet areas.

CAPRIFOLIACEAE - Honeysuckle Family
Elderberry *(Sambucus canadensis)* when controlled in a lawn situation produces large showy clusters of flowers and fruits. The fruits are choice food of songbirds and can be used to make jelly. Snowberry *(Symphoriocarpus orbiculatus)* produces small white flowers and pink fruits. The viburnums *(Viburnum acerifolium, V. dentatum, V. nudum, and V. rufidulum)* produce showy clusters of white flowers and blue fruits.

CELASTRACEAE - Stafftree Family
Strawberry bush *(Euonymus americanus)* produces showy clusters of fruits with red seeds. The bittersweet vine *(Celastrus scandens)* produces similar seeds.

137

CLETHRACEAE - Clethra Family
Blackpepper bush *(Clethra alnifolia)* - showy white flowers.

CORNACEAE - Dogwood Family
Flowering dogwood *(Cornus florida)* - showy white bracts and red fruits.
Swamp dogwood *(Cornus stricta)* - tiny flowers and blue fruits.
Roughleaf dogwood *(Cornus drummondii)* - small flowers and white fruits.

CYRILLACEAE - Titi Family
Titi *(Cyrilla racemiflora)* - showy clusters of white flowers.
Buckwheat tree *(Cliftonia monophylla)* - fragrant showy white flowers.

ERICACEAE - Heath Family
Mountain laurel *(Kalmia latifolia)* - evergreen; showy flowers.
Sweetbells *(Leucothoe racemiflora)* - bell-shaped white flowers; deciduous.
Doghobble *(Leucothoe axillaria)* - evergreen; white flowers.
He-huckleberry *(Lyonia ligustrina* and *Lyonia mariana)* - white flowers.
Fetterbush *(Lyonia lucida)* - evergreen; showy flowers.
Sourwood *(Oxydendrum arboreum)* Lily-of-the-valley type flowers; excellent fall color.
Wild azaleas *(Rhododendron oblongifolium)* - white flowers.
    (R. canescens and R. viscosum) - pink flowers.
Blueberries *(Vaccinium arkansanum, V. darrowii, V. elliottii, V. virgatum)* - edible fruits.
Farkleberries *(Vaccinium arborem)* - large shrub with showy white flowers.
Deerberries *(Vaccinium stamineum)* - excellent sour fruit for jellies.
Huckleberries *(Gaylussacia dumosa* and *G. mosieri)* - small; edible fruits.
Ericaceous plants require acid soils. Most can be started from stem cuttings using rooting hormones and mist systems.

FABACEAE - Bean Family
Acacia *(Acacia smallii)* - dissected, fern-like leaves; white flowers.
Redbud *(Cercis canadensis)* - showy flowers; beautiful leaves.
Blacklocust *(Robinia pseudoacacia)* - Wisteria-like white flowers.

138

HAMAMELIDACEAE - Witch Hazel Family
Witch hazel *(Hamamelis virginiana)* - yellow flowers in November.

HIPPOCASTANEACEAE - Horsechestnut Family
Red Buckeye *(Aesculus pavia)* - showy red flowers; unique leaves.

HYPERICACEAE - St. John's Wort Family
Hypericum (several species of *Hypericum*) - showy yellow flowers.

LAMIACEAE - Mint Family
Georgia Calamint *(Calamintha georgiana)* - small shrub with pink flowers.

LAURACEAE - Laurel Family
Spicebush *(Lindera benzoin)* - highly scented stem and leaves.
Redbay *(Persea palustris)* - evergreen leaves used as "bay" leaves.
Sassafras *(Sassafras albidum)* - showy yellow flowers before leaves.

MAGNOLIACEAE - Magnolia Family
Most Louisiana species make tree-sized plants but are included because of their desirability as "flowering" woody plants.
Cucumber magnolia *(Magnolia acuminata)* - lemon-scented flowers.
Pyramid magnolia *(Magnolia pyramidata)* - showy flowers and leaves.
Big-leaf magnolia *(Magnolia macrophylla)* - very large flowers and leaves.
Virginia Bay magnolia *(Magnolia virginiana)* - partially evergreen.
Southern magnolia *(Magnolia grandiflora)* - flowers and evergreen leaves.
Tulip tree, Yellow poplar *(Liriodendron tulipifera)* - prettiest flowers and leaves among our native plants.
Florida Anise *(Illicium floridanum)* - evergreen fragrant leaves; red flowers. Only true shrub in this family in Louisiana.

MYRICACEAE - Wax-Myrtle Family
Wax myrtle *(Myrica cerifera* and *M. heterophylla)* - easily grown, evergreen plant that is easily pruned to any desired shape.
Odorless bayberry *(Myrica inodora)* - small with specialized habitat.

OLEACEAE - Olive or Ash Family
Greybeard or Fringe tree *(Chionanthus virginicus)* - showy flowers.

Devilwood *(Osmanthus americanus)* - evergreen.

Ashes *(Fraxinus americana, F. caroliniana, F. pennsylvanica* and *F. profunda)* - tree-sized plants.

The widespread shrubby pest, privet *(Ligustrum sp.)*, is in this family.

POLYGONACEAE - Buckwheat Family
American jointstem *(Polygonella americana)* - small shrub with massive sprays of small white flowers.

RHAMNACEAE - Buckthorn Family
New Jersey Tea *(Ceanothus americanus)* -small shrub with white flowers.

Indian Cherry *(Rhamnus caroliniana)* - shining leaves; showy fruits.

ROSACEAE - Rose Family
Serviceberry *(Amelanchier arborea)* - very pretty leaves; edible fruits. Showy early flowers.

Hawthorne *(Crataegus sp.)* - excellent shape; showy flowers and fruits.

Mayhaw *(Crataegus opaca)* - showy flowers; edible fruits.

Chickasaw Plum *(Prunus angustifolia)* - desirable fruits.

Bigtree Plum *(Prunus americana; P. mexicana)* - white flowers; edible fruit.

Sloes *(Prunus umbellata)* - edible fruits.

Sand Plum *(Prunus gracilis)* - small shrub for dry areas.

Wild crabapples *(Pyrus angustifolia)* - showy flowers; edible fruits.

Chokeberry *(Pyrus arbutifolia)* - showy flowers and fruits.

Roses *(Rosa carolina, R. laevigata, R. bractaeta)* - flowers.

RUBIACEAE - Madder Family
Buttonbush (Cephalanthus Occidentalis) - showy balls of flowers.

RUTACEAE - Citrus Family
Toothache Tree *(Zanthoxylum clava-herculis)* - pleasant shape; unique bark.

Northern Prickly Ash *(Zanthoxylum americanum)* - clump-forming shrub.

SAPINDACEAE - Soapberry Family
Western Soapberry *(Sapindus saponaria)* - compound leaves.

SAPOTACEAE - Sapodilla Family
Chittim wood *(Bumelia lanuginosa)* and others - sturdy, adaptable.

SAXIFRAGACEAE - Saxifrage Family
Virginia willow *(Itea virginica)* - fragrant flowers, showy fall foliage.
Oakleaf Hydrangea *(Hydrangea quercifolia)* - attractive leaves and long-lasting bracts; very wide range of tolerance of soils.
Hydrangea *(Hydrangea arborescens)* - rare but easily cultivated.

STYRACACEAE - Storax Family
Snowbells *(Styrax americana* and *S. grandiflora)* - showy white flowers.
Silverbells *(Halesia diptera)* - showy white flowers; attractive bark.

SYMPLOCACEAEA - Sweetleaf family
Sweetleaf *(Symplocos tinctoria)* - evergreen; yellow flowers.

TAMARICACEA - Tamarisk Family
Tamarisk *(Tamarix gallica)* - Cedar-like foliage; pink flowers.

THYMEAELACEAE - Leatherwood Family
Leatherwood *(Dirca palustris)* - small shrub; flowers in February.

ULMACEAE - Elm Family
Elms *(Ulmus alata, U. americana, U. crassifolia)* - trees.
Hackberry *(Celtis laevigata)* - excellent in coastal areas.
Dwarf hackberry *(Celtis tenuifolia)* - stays shrub-sized.
Water elm *(Planera aquatica)* - unique shape; small leaves.

VERBENACEAE - Verbena Family
French Mulberry or American Beautyberry *(Callicarpa americana)* - beautiful flowers and fruits. A white-berried form can be propagated by cuttings.

Dr. R. Dale Thomas
Director of the NLU Herbarium
Department of Biology
Northeast Louisiana University
Monroe, LA

Roses

Roses require too much care! Roses won't grow for me! They get little blackspots all over the leaves. What is your favorite flower? A rose . . . of course.

How in the world the nursery industry could allow the consumer to become so turned off to the world's favorite flower and now our National Flower will always be a mystery to me. While roses do require some extra care, so does everything else we grow - azaleas, camellias, all sorts of bedding plants, yes, and even grass.

Usually, when things are done half way, one winds up doing them all over again, many times doubling the labor and time involved. Hopefully, this brief outline on rose growing will make growing roses a fulfilling and rewarding endeavor for anyone who follows it. If you don't follow every part, don't go around telling everyone how difficult rose growing is.

Roses are a high light intensity crop. They require at least six hours of sun daily. Morning sun up until about 3:00 in the afternoon is ideal. All day sun in July and August is hard on roses and will reduce their growth during this period. They will cook to a crisp as will almost anything else. However, if they are kept watered and disease free, they will survive in good shape. Don't plant them where they are shaded until mid-afternoon.

Raised beds are much preferred for roses as well as bedding plants. Drainage is absolutely necessary. Beds raised from 4 to 6 inches are fine. Dig deep beds one shovel deep and place soil to one side. Mix good sandy topsoil with the soil removed. In other words, add a layer of sandy topsoil and roto-till; add a layer of the soil removed and roto-till, etc. , until you have built the bed up to the desired height. If you want to add organic matter such as pine bark, peat moss, leaves, etc., it's o.k. Please, no gin trash!

After the bed is prepared, take a sampling of soil from several areas, mix it togther, and place at least one pint in a plastic bag. Take it to your Cooperative Extension Service for testing. This will tell you how much lime to add to your bed. Samples should be taken yearly in the fall for lime recommendations. If you refuse to take soil samples, add 10 lbs. of lime per 100 square feet of bed space.

PLEASE set up some type of watering system that is simple. No hose dragging! There are countless ways to water that are

inexpensive, simple, and long lasting. Ask your local nurseryman for help.

Bareroot roses should be planted by March 1 in Northeast Louisiana. Potted plants may be planted anytime of the year. Plant the bud union (knot, lump) at ground level. Don't disturb the roots on potted plants. On bareroot plants, make a cone in the bottom of the hole to support the roots. Water the plants after planting.

Mulch your bed after planting. Mulching conserves moisture and reduces or eliminates weeds. You won't grow good roses if they are having to compete with grass. If you have to pull it out, the roses are going to require too much care. The mulch should be thick, at least 4 inches. Good mulches are pine straw, clean pine bark, and cotton seed hulls. Cotton seed hulls are used for cattle feed. This is not gin trash. It can be obtained from feed and seed stores. If the cotton seed hulls become crusty, break them up with a rake or hoe.

Feed your roses as soon as you plant your bed and be consistent in doing it. Use no systemic insecticides and fertilizer combinations. Systemics cause hardening of the plants and blind shoots. Fertilize with special rose foods according to the label instructions or use the following:

1. *Ammonium nitrate* - 1 lb/100 sq. ft. monthly.

2. *13-13-13 or 8-8-8* - 2 lbs/100 sq ft. monthly.

3. *Epsom salts* (for magnesium) - 2 lbs/100 sq. ft. in spring and mid-summer.

Apply the ammonium nitrate at the first of the month and the 13-13-13 or 8-8-8 at the middle of the month. Never fertilize dry plants, and water in the fertilizer immediately - no need to remove the mulch. Stop feeding about October 1.

Spraying is a necessity to grow good roses. Early spring and fall are the most important times for spraying. Blackspot is prevalent during the rainy season. Unless it is controlled, it will defoliate your bushes and leave you roseless. There are many excellent sprays available for control of fungus and insects. Add a non-ionic spreader-sticker to your mixture. If it rains the day after you spray, you won't have to spray the next day. Be sure the spreader-sticker is non-ionic or your foliage will burn. Spray every 7-10 days.

Many spray materials are compatible and can all be mixed together. Read the labels!

Never cut long stems on newly planted bushes. Let them go through at least two bloom cycles before you cut long stems. This will let the new bush become established and develop lots of leaves for foodmaking. On established bushes, cut blooms down to about one-half of the stem length. Never cut off more than 2/3 of the flowering stem. For years a rule of thumb with roses has been to cut to the first five-leaflet leaf. That's too short on established bushes. Always cut to strong wood.

Cut correctly

Cut too high

Cut too near bud

Pruning established bushes should be done around Washington's Birthday. Cut out all dead wood flush to the bud union and any small, lanky growth. Prune canes just above a dormant bud-eye (about 1/4 inch). Canes should be pruned to about 18 inches. Begin your fertilizer and spray programs then.

One of the largest growth areas in the rose industry is with miniature roses. They are available in a variety of colors and have unlimited use in the landscape. They can be used as borders, in mass plantings, hanging baskets, cascading ground covers, or in pots. General care is the same as for the larger flowering types. However, because miniatures are smaller, have more foliage, and are usually freer blooming, their care requirements are less.

Pot growing of miniatures will require more care due to having to water more frequently. They may be planted into 10-12 inch pots and moved wherever you need color at the time. They can be brought inside for 3-4 days and then moved back outside. When growing roses in pots, you must use a good soil mix. Don't expect to grow miniatures or anything else in $1.49 per 50 lbs. junk. Liquid fertilizer is good for pot growing.

144

The following is a list of rose varieties that are hardy, free-blooming, vigorous, and very easy to grow - easy if you follow directions well.

HYBRID TEAS
(large flowered)

Red
*Olympiad
*Mr. Lincoln
*Royal Canadian

White
Pascali
White Masterpiece
Sheer Bliss

Orange
*Fragrant Cloud
*Touch of Class

Pink
*Friendship
*Tiffany

Mauve
Blue Nile

Yellow
Peace
King's Ransom

Bicolor
Alabama
Color Magic
*Double Delight
*Granada

FLORIBUNDAS
(bloom in sprays)

Red
Europeana

Mauve
Deep Purple
*Angel Face

Bicolor
Double Talk

Orange
First Edition

Pink
Cherish

Yellow
Sunsprite
Sunflare

White
Ivory Fashion

MINIATURE ROSES

Red
B.C.
Black Jade
Charlie
New Orleans

Bicolor
Prairie Schooner
Magic Carrousel
Charmglo
*Heartlight

Yellow
Rise 'n Shine
Rainbow's End

White
Pace Setter
Jet Trail

Pink
Teedelum
Peaches 'n Cream

Orange
Speechless
Julie Ann
Petite Foile

Mauve
Winsome
*Lavender Jade
*Sachet
Lavender Jewel

denotes fragrance

145

There is a tremendous amount of breeding being done by rose breeders in Europe and the United States. Over the next ten years we will see all different types of roses being introduced - from continuous blooming, creeping, climbing, crawling, falling roses to miniature roses that will grow extremely compact, be very disease resistant, and bloom and bloom and bloom.

As a last word, buy good quality, healthy plants. Make sure your plants are well watered. Flood the bed at least two times a week during June, July, and August. Be consistent! If you stop spraying and caring for your bushes, don't expect prize winning roses in 30 days.

Benson Eugene King
Rose Grower
Past President, Monroe Chapter
American Rose Society
Monroe, LA

Care of Cut
Materials

Care of Cut Material

In Sandra Hynson's *Homage Through Flowers*, she says, "The care and preservation of cut flowers is as important a study as the mechanics and placement of flowers themselves."

Flower arrangers and gardeners are interested in the care of cut material. This involves cutting and conditioning (hardening). One of the pitfalls is bacterial growth; to avoid this, use very clean tools: buckets, knives, shears, and containers that have been washed and soaked in bleach.

Another problem is that when flowers are cut a callous forms on the cut, trapping an air bubble which blocks water absorption. Some experts recut then dip the end of the flower in almost boiling water for a minute or two to push the air bubble out. The Japanese recommend recutting the stem under water to avoid air seal.

In general, flowers should be picked just before they reach their peak. Cut the stems on a wide slant with a very sharp knife or shears. Using a wide angle allows the tip to rest on the bottom of the container, leaving the exposed area free to absorb water.

Flowers are best when cut in the late afternoon or early morning. Many experts prefer late afternoon. Avoid the noonday sun. Strip any leaves that will be underwater since foliage decays quickly. Place the flower in the well-scrubbed bucket of water. To harden, leave the flowers in a cool, shady place at least one hour, preferably overnight.

Tip: One part water to one part lemon-lime soda (not diet) will keep material fresh longer.

Annuals and Perennials

COMMON NAME	COLORS	BLOOM TIME	CONDITIONING TIPS
Abelia	White	Summer	Break stem. Soak in warm water.
Acanthus Bear's Breech	Mauve and white	Summer	Leaves or blossoms. Singe or boil then cond.
Ageratum	White, blue, rose	June to frost	Cut half open. Cond. in warm water and sugar.
Amaryllis	White, red, pink, orange, salmon or bicolor	Fall to spring	Cut on slant as bud opens, fill stems with water, and plug them.
Anemone	Red, white, blue, pink	Spring	Cond. in boiling water briefly. Cold water soak overnight.
Aster	Lavender, blue, white, pink, rose	Summer to fall	Condition in hot water, then condition overnight in 1 qt. water with 1 tsp. sugar.
Astilbe	white, pink, red, lavender	May - June	Cut 3/4 open; put in cold water.
Baby's Breath *Gypsophila*	White	February-May	Cut when about half the flowers are open.
Bachelor's Button	White, blue, purple, pink	February-May	Cond. in cold water.
Balloon Flower	White, blue	June-October	"
Beard Tongue *Penstemon*	White, pink, red	May - June	Split stems. Cond. in cold water.
Bee Balm	Red, rose, pink	May - June	Cut when 1/2 open. Cond. in warm water with 1 tsp. sugar.
Belladonna Lily *Amaryllis belladonna*	Rose pink	July - September	Cond. in cool water.

150

COMMON NAME	COLORS	BLOOM TIME	CONDITIONING TIPS
Bellflower *Campanula*	Purple, white, blue, lavender	Early summer to frost depending on variety	Split stems; put in boiling water 2-3 min.
Bells of Ireland	Green	Summer	Submerge in cold water two hours.
Bergenia	Pink, white	March, April	Cold water 3 to 4 hours.
Blanketflower *Gaillardia*	Yellow, red, orange, bicolor	Early summer to frost	Split stems. Cond. with l tsp. sugar to l qt. water.
Blazing Star Gay feather *Liatris*	White, purple	Mid to late summer	Scrape last inch or two of stem and make cross cuts.
Bleeding Heart	Pink	Early summer	Split stems; put in cold water.
Bugloss	Blue	April	"
Buttercup *Ranunculus*	Yellow	Summer	Split stems. Cond. in hot water with sugar.
Butterfly Lily *Hedychium coronarium*	White	Late summer	Cond. in cool shallow water.
Calendula	Yellow, orange	March - May; October - December	" Remove all foliage below water level.
Calla Lily *Zantedeschia*	White, yellow	Spring and summer	Cond. in cool water. Split stems; wrap with floral tape. Submerge foliage l or 2 hours.
Canna Lily *Canna*	Red, yellow, orange, pink, bicolor	May - November	Submerge leaves in water overnight.

COMMON NAME	COLORS	BLOOM TIME	CONDITIONING TIPS
Candytuft	White, red, lavender	November - May	Cut 1/2 open, split stems, and put in warm water.
Carnation	White, pink, yellow, orange, lavender	Early summer, fall, and spring	Place stem in water with 1/2 tsp. boric acid to 2 qts. water.
Christmas Rose *Heleborus niger*	White to greenish	Late winter and early spring	Split stems; put in cold water.
Chrysanthemum	White, pink, yellow, lavender, bronze, wine	Late summer to frost	Cond. in water at room temperature with 1/2 c. sugar to 1 qt. water.
Cockscomb *Celosia*	Red, yellow, bronze, bicolor	June - November	" May be dried.
Columbine	Many colors	Spring	Stems in oil of peppermint. Cond. in water at room temperature.
Coreopsis	Yellow brown center	Summer	Cond. in cold water with 1 tsp. salt to 1 qt. water.
Coneflower	Rose copper center	Summer	"
Cosmos Early Late	Pink, lavender, yellow	April - July; August - October	" Select flowers whose pollen hasn't yet developed.
Crinum	White, pink, wine	Late spring, summer	Cond. in cool, shallow water.
Daffodil *Narcissus*	White, yellow	February - April	Cut newly opened flowers, split stems slightly, recut under warm water. Cond. in deep cold water.

COMMON NAME	COLORS	BLOOM TIME	CONDITIONING TIPS
Dahlia	All but blue and green	Midsummer to fall	Soak in cold water for l hour, then in boiling water with a few drops of alcohol.
Daisy *Daisy*	White yellow center	May - June	Room temp. water with 8 drops peppermint oil to l gal. of water. Remove all leaves below water level.
Black-eyed susan	Yelow, black, or brown center	Summer	"
English Daisy	White, pink	Spring	"
Shasta	White yellow center	June - October	Burn stems or place in hot water
Daylily *Hemerocallis*	All but blue	Summer	Cut in bud - only lasts one day.
Dusty Miller	Silver foliage	Summer	Split ends and cond. in hot water.
Easter Lily	White	Late spring	Split stems. Cond. in cold water.
False Dragon-head	Pink, white	Late summer, early fall	Soak in warm water.
False Indigo	Blue, yellow	Spring	Cut l/2 open, split stems. Cond. in warm water and sugar.
Feverfew	White yellow center	June	Cut stems. Cond. in warm water and sugar.
Flowering Onion *Allium*	White, lavender, blue	Spring	Cut as buds open. Can dry.
Foxglove *Digitalis*	White, pink, purple, yellow	Spring	Cut when l/4 open. Cond. in warm water.

COMMON NAME	COLORS	BLOOM TIME	CONDITIONING TIPS
Geranium	White, red, orange, pink, bicolor	Late spring	Remove leaves below water.
Gladiolus	Bicolor, red, yellow, orange, white, purple	Late spring, early summer	Use sugar in cold water to soak.
Gloriosa	Yellow, orange, gold, mahogany	Summer	Deep tepid water.
Globe Thistle	Bluish-grey	Summer	Split stems. Cond. in warm water.
Goats Beard	White, pink		Cond. in warm water and sugar.
Golden Spider Lily *Lycoris Africana*	Yellow	September	Cond. in cool water.
Hollyhock	Pink, red, purple, white, yellow	Summer	Fill, plug stems. Place stem in very hot water for 1 minute.
Hyacinth *Hyacinth*	White, purple, blue, yellow, orange, lavender	March, April	Cond. in cool water.
H. Galtonia	White	June - July	"
H. Romanus	White, blue	March	" First to bloom.
Iris Dutch	Blue, copper, yellow	Spring	Cut when bud is about to open. Cond. in water at room temperature.
Bearded	White, purple	Spring	"
Louisiana	Bronze, blue, yellow, white	Spring	" Valuable for strap-like foliage.

COMMON NAME	COLORS	BLOOM TIME	CONDITIONING TIPS
Jupiter's Beard	White, pink, red	Year-round, early summer, mid-fall	Split woody stems. Cond. in cold water.
Kaffir Lily *Clivia*	Orange to scarlet	Spring	Cut 1/2 open. Cond. in cold water.
Larkspur	White, blue, pink, purple	March - June	1/2 tsp. wood alcohol to 2 qts. water.
Lenten Rose *Helleborus orientalis*	White, lavender, green	Early-mid spring	Singe or scald stems.
Loosestrife *Lythrum*	Pink, magenta	Summer	Strip foliage. Cond. in warm water.
Oriental Poppy	Scarlet to orange, pink	Summer	Singe stem ends or dip in boiling water. Cond. in cold water; then arrange in water with sugar.
Peony	White, pink, rose, variegated	Early spring	Split ends. Cond. in 1 qt. water with 3 tsps. sugar.
Pinks Sweet William *Dianthus*	Purple, red, pink, rose, white, mauve, or bicolor	Summer	Cut stem at a slant above joints and split larger stems.
Plantain Lily *Hosta*	Pale or deep blue, lavender to white	Summer	Split stems and cond. in cold water. Cut when 3 or 4 flowers open. Foliage valuable.
Ranunculus	Pink, orange, yellow, red, white	Spring	Cut 3/4 open; split stems. Cond. in cold water.
Red -Hot-Poker	Red, yellow, orange, ivory	Late summer, fall, and winter	Cut 1/2 open. Cond. in cold water.

COMMON NAME	COLORS	BLOOM TIME	CONDITIONING TIPS
Ressurection Lily *Lycoris radiata*	Red	September - October	Cool water.
Salvia	Red, blue	April - frost	Cut; place in cool water.

Scabiosa
  Pincushion
  Flower
	Blue,
	lavender
		Summer	Split stems; remove
			leaves. Cond. in cold
			water.

Scilla	White, pink, blue	Early spring	Do not cut white part. Soak in warm water.
Sedum Stonecrop	Pink, ivory, red	Late summer, fall	Cond. in cold water. Cut when 1/2 open.
Snapdragon	White, pink, red, yellow, bronze	Early Summer	To 1 qt. of hot water add 3 tsp. sugar and 2 tsp. white distilled vinegar or submerge 1/2 hour in cold water - overnight in warm water. Do not mist.
Snow Drops *Galanthus nivalis*	White	March	"
Spider Lily *Hymenocallis littoralis H. accidentalis Lycoris Radiata*	White; coral, red	Late spring, summer; August - September	Cond. in cool water.
Spiderwort *Tradescant*	Blue, pink	Spring	Cut; place in warm water.
Stock	Pink, white, rose, yellow rose, rust	February - May	Strip stem with veg. peeler. Soak in warm water.
Stokes' Aster *Stokesia*	Blue, lavender	Summer	Split stems; remove leaves below water level. Cond. in water with 1 tsp. sugar per qt.
Sunflower	Yellow	July - September	"

COMMON NAME	COLORS	BLOOM TIME	CONDITIONING TIPS
Sweet Pea	Var. colors	January - March	Re-cut stems under water. To warm water add l tsp. alcohol per l qt. water.
Tuberose	White	July - August, summer	Cond. in cool water.
Tulip	Many colors	Spring	Cut when buds are ready to open; split stems. Cond. in warm water with l tsp. gin to l pint water in deep cold water to strengthen.
Verbena	White, purple, red, blue, pink	January - December	Cut when partially open. Cond. briefly in boiling water with l/2 tsp. sugar added per qt. - overnight in cool water.
Violet	Blue, purple, white, rose	Late winter, spring	Submerge stems and flowers in cold water for l to 2 hours.
Watsonia	White, red, pink, lavender	Summer	Cond. in cool water.
Yarrow	Yellow, pink, white	Summer	2 Tbls. of salt to l qt. water. Pick when flowers are l/2 open. Good to dry.
Zinnia	All but blue, multicolor	May - November	Cut when not quite open; remove foliage. Cond. in cold water- take water to garden when cutting.

Trees, Vines, Shrubs

COMMON NAME	COLORS	BLOOM TIME	CONDITIONING TIPS
Almond	Pink	Spring	Split stems.
Azalea	Orange, red, pink, lavender, white	Spring	Put stems in 2" of boiling water to which 1 jigger of gin is added.
Bridal Wreath *Spiraea*	White	Spring	Split stems. Cond. in warm water with 1 tsp. sugar to 1 qt. water, then cold water overnight.
Butterfly Bush *Buddleia*	Lavender, white	Summer	Cut when 1/2 open; split stems. Cond. in warm water.
Camellia	Red, white, pink, bi-color	Winter	Cut and split stems when flowers are open.
Candlestick Tree	Yellow	Late summer - fall	Split stems.
Cherry	White, pink	Spring	Cut when 1/4 open. Remove foliage. Split stems. Cond. in cold water.
Clematis	Pink, white, blue, lavender	Summer	Split stems if woody. Cond. in glass of cold water to which 1 jigger of gin is added.
Crab, Flowering	Pink, white, red	Spring	Split stems. Cond. in cold water with 5 drops of hydrochloric acid to 1 qt. water.
Crape Myrtle	Watermelon red, lavender, white, pink, rose	Summer	Break stem. Place in tepid water.
Deutsia	White	Spring	Split stems. Cond. in warm water.

COMMON NAME	COLORS	BLOOM TIME	CONDITIONING TIPS
Dogwood	White, pink, red	Spring	Break stem. Add 3 or 4 drops hydrochloric acid to 1 qt. water. Soak 8 hours in warm water.
Forsythia	Yellow	Spring	(a) Cut just below a node. Cond. in cold water. (b) To force, put in hot water near window or in good light.
Gardenia	White	Summer	Break stem. Harden in cool water. Do not touch blossom.
Hibiscus	Yellow, red, pink, orange	Summer	One day flower.
Hydrangea	White, blue, pink	Late spring - early summer	Singe stems or put in very hot water. Sub- merge wilted flower heads in warm water to revive.
Honeysuckle	Red, white		Split stems. Cond. in cold water.
Jasmine Carolina	Yellow	Spring	Put stems in 1 pt. boiling water with 2 tsp. gin for 2 minutes. Cond. in cold water.
Gelsemium sempervirens	"	"	"
Confederate	White	"	"
Trachelosperum jasminoides	"	"	"
Magnolia *Magnolia grandiflora*	White	Late spring	Cut in full bud. Split stems. Submerge in cold water briefly. Submerge again before arrang- ing. Wrap in damp kleenex to prevent opening.

Care of Cut Materials - Trees, Vine, Shrubs, continued

COMMON NAME	COLORS	BLOOM TIME	CONDITIONING TIPS
Magnolia Stellata	White	Late Spring	Cut in full bud. Split stems. Submerge in cold water briefly. Submerge again before arranging. Wrap in damp kleenex to prevent opening.
Chinese *Magnolia denudata*	White, pink, purplish	Early spring	Cut when buds are about to open. Cross split stems
Chinese *Magnolia soulangiana*	"	"	"
Sweet Bay *Magnolia virginiana*	White	Late spring	"
Japanese Maple *Acer*	Reddish Foliage only	Spring and fall	Split stems. Put in l qt. water with 2 tsp. sugar.
Mock Orange	White	Spring	Cut when blossom is 1/4 open. Split stem and cond. in warm water.
Morning Glory	White, pink, blue	Summer	Cut in bud. Crush stems. Rub with salt. Do not use metal container.
Oleander	White, rose, peach	Summer	Cut when bloom is 1/2 open. Split stem and singe. Cond. in warm water.
Peach	White, pink	Spring	Split stems. Cond. in l pt. water with several drops of hydrochloric acid for 1 minute. Cold water for 8 hours.

COMMON NAME	COLORS	BLOOM TIME	CONDITIONING TIPS
Pear	White	Spring	Split stems. Cond. in 1 qt. water with 3 or 4 drops hydrochloric acid.
Pearl Bush	White	Early spring	Split stem. Warm water.
Plum	Pink, white	Spring	Split stem. Warm water.
Pussy Willow	Pinkish grey catkins	Spring	Split stems. Cut when less than half catkins are open.
Pyracantha	White flowers, red berries	Spring; fall	Split stems. Warm water.
Quince, Flowering	Red, pink, coral, white	Winter - early spring	Split stems. Cond. in warm water and sugar. Easily forced.
Raphiolepsis Indian Hawthorn	White or Pink	Summer	Split stems. Warm water.
R. umbellata	"	"	"
Redbud	Reddish pink	Spring	Split stems. Cond. in l qt. warm water with l T. sugar.
Rose	Bi and multi-colors, all but blue and purple	Spring - fall	Cut at a wide angle with knife above a 5 leaflet leaf. Soak in deep warm water to which 3 tsp. sugar, 3 Tblsp. vinegar, and 3 tsp. bleach per quart have been added. Use same water for arrangement.
Rose of Sharon *Althea*	white to rose to lavender	July - August	One day flower. l tsp. sugar to l qt. water. Mist blooms.
Scotch Broom	yellow or white	May - frost	Split stem and cond. in warm water.

161

Care of Cut Materials - Trees, Vine, Shrubs, continued

COMMON NAME	COLORS	BLOOM TIME	CONDITIONING TIPS
Viburnum Snowball	White	Spring	Split stem and cond. in warm water.
V. carlcephalum	"	"	"
V. plicatum maries	"	"	"
Weigela	Rose pink	May	Cond. in warm water with 3 tsp. sugar per qt.
Wisteria	Lavender, white	Spring	Split stems. Add 3 tsp. sugar per qt. of water.
Yucca	White	Mid-summer	Cut stems. Warm water.

Garden Foliage for Flower Arrangements

Abelia
Aucuba
Aspidistra
Azalea
Banksia rose trails
Bamboo
Boxwood
Bush Honeysuckle
Caladium
Camellia
Canna
Cedar
Cherry Laurel
Croton
Dogwood
Elaeagnus
Eucalyptus
Euonymus
Fatsia

Forsythia
Ferns
Hollies
Hosta
Gardenia
Ivy
Iris foliage
Jasmine Trails
Juniper
Ligustrum
Laurel
Magnolia
Myrtle
Nandina
Pachysandra
Palmetto
Palms
Pearl bush
Photinia

Pine
Pineapple Guava
Pittosporum
Plum
Pomegranate
Pussy Willow (*and other Willows*)
Sasanqua
Sourwood
Spiraea
Smilax
Viburnum
Vitex
Weigela
Yew
Yaupon
Yucca

These are excellent choices for receptions and altar arrangements. Add garden foliage to florist flowers to soften them and to express creativeness.

General Rules for Foliage Conditioning

Foliage material is cut and conditioned much the same way as is described for flowers; knives or pruning shears must be sharp, containers clean, and material allowed to harden in water for several hours or overnight.

If possible, avoid cutting foliage that has new growth on the branches, as these tender leaves wilt easily. The new growth may be pinched off the branch, providing that this pinching will not destroy the line of the branch to be used.

Some foliage material requires special treatment for proper water intake or to retain peak condition:

Woody branches - remove leaves from the portion which will extend below the water line of your container, split the ends, and place in warm water (e.g. forsythia, mock orange, aucuba.)

Stems with milky or colorless fluid - remove leaves that will be below water line, split stem, and place in very hot water, being sure to protect any leaves or flower heads (these can be wrapped in newspaper). Another method is to hold the stems over a candle or the burner on the stove, searing them before placing in warm water (e.g. hydrangeas). **Never** allow hot water to touch foliage to be used in your arrangement, as it is quickly damaged.

Caladiums, Hostas, Ferns - cut with a sharp knife. After selecting stems sturdy enough to support leaves, split stems and condition overnight in cold water. If leaves seem soft, submerge in cold water for about 1/2 hour or more until crisp **before** conditioning.

These rules are very general. Foliage can be cut earlier than flowers and keeps longer. Remember, nothing is prettier than an all green arrangement!

Mélange

French. A mixture or medley.

Good Garden Practices:
Leave rake tines and hoe edges pointed down.
Wear heavy shoes for mowing and digging.
Keep children out of the area when mowing.
Keep chemicals out of the reach of small children.
Beware of plants that are poisonous.

Herbs

Speak out, whisper not
Here bloweth thyme and bergamot
Softly on thee every hour
Secret herbs their spices shower.

Walter de la Mare

Herbs are fun to grow, fragrant, helpful, and beautiful. They can be planted in pots, vegetable gardens, and perennial borders. Herb gardens can be formal or informal in design. With a little soil preparation, good drainage, and sun, they are a gardener's delight. Even weeding is fun in the herb garden; good scents surround the gardener, bees buzz happily, thoughts of delicious dinners flavored with rosemary, basil, and thyme float through the weeder's head and make work light.

Herbs like at least five hours of sun a day and loose, well-drained soil. To prepare the bed, dig down 12 to 18 inches and add organic material like peat moss and manure, or compost if it is available; river sand can also be added if the soil is heavy clay. A good soil mix is 3 parts compost, 2 parts sand, and 1 part peat moss. A soil that is slightly alkaline is important for good growth, and lime should be added to bring the soil to a pH of 6.5 to 7.5, if necessary. If the soil needs phosphorous, add 4 to 5 pounds of bone meal for every 100 feet. The soil does not need to be too rich, as the plants are more flavorful in a slightly poor soil. Manure and compost are good fertilizers for herbs; they really do not need anything stronger. Border the beds with bricks or landscape timbers that have not been treated with creosote, which is toxic to plants.

Mulch is very important in the herb garden as it provides weed control, holds moisture in the soil, and keeps the plants clean. Mulch can be hay, cottonseed hulls, straw, pine needles, or whatever material is available. A pretty bed can be made by using pine bark nuggets on top of a 4 to 6 inch mulch.

Herbs are somewhat resistant to insects, but if an invasion has occurred, spray with a garlic and cayenne pepper mixture. If this does not work and the plants are being destroyed, use a commercial spray but do not harvest plant material with residue on the leaves for potpourri. Slugs can be controlled with shallow dishes or grapefruit halves filled with beer placed in the garden and thrown away when full.

SPRING is the time to plant the garden, having first pulled the winter mulch away and making sure the dead stems have

been pruned back. Be careful to wait long enough for spring growth to occur before doing any severe pruning or discarding of plants which appear to be dead.

There are several ways to start plants besides simply sowing seeds in the beds or buying small potted plants at the local garden center. Root division of older plants can be done by digging them up, pulling or cutting them apart, and replanting. Cuttings can be made by cutting a 4 inch sprig from a well-grown perennial just below a leaf joint, taking off the bottom leaves, and planting in a pot or flat filled with moist sand or peat moss. A rooting hormone is helpful for stimulating growth. Another way to start plants is to sow seeds inside six weeks before the plants should be set out. Sow the seeds in flats filled with fine sphagnum moss, barely covering them with another layer of moss and keeping them moist, not soggy. Cover the flat with plastic and put in a warm place until the first growth occurs. Move them to a sunny window, removing the plastic; then plant in small pots filled with sterile potting soil when the first leaves appear. Do not let them dry out. Plant them in the garden after the last frost date.

SUMMER is harvesting time in the garden. Plants can be harvested two or three times in Zone 8 as there is a long growing season. Harvest in the early morning when the dew has dried on the leaves before the sun is too hot, always leaving at least one-third of the plant's foliage. Dry leaves and seeds in a cool, dry place, either hanging in bunches or laying flat on screens. This should be done out of the sun. As soon as the leaves are crisp and dry, place them in jars with tight lids, labeling them carefully. Herbs can also be frozen by washing the leaves, drying them thoroughly and freezing them in labeled plastic bags. Jellies and vinegars can be made now along with potpourri for holiday gifts.

Maintaining the garden in summer calls for weeding, pest control, and pinching back annuals to keep them from flowering as they will go to seed and die if this is not done. In times of high humidity, watch for disease such as mildew or other fungi and use an appropriate fungicide, following the directions explicitly.

Early FALL is a good time to pot plants which should be brought inside for the winter. Tender perennials such as bay, lemon verbena, and scented geraniums need to be brought inside and wintered in a sunny window. Place the plants in pots filled with fresh potting soil, and after watering thoroughly, trim back and place them in a shady spot. This is also a good time to plant perennials as this allows plants to become established before the hot summer arrives. Garlic can be planted now. Plant each garlic

clove pointed end up in a spot that gets full sun.

WINTER is the time to care for the herbs living indoors. They need to be inspected for pests, kept cool at night, and watered well. Do not let the roots stand in excess water. Fertilize them with a weak fish emulsion when they are first brought in and again in late winter or early spring. Try to give them enough light in a sunny window, and if the light is not enough, try artificial light. In the garden, leaves make a good winter cover which should be raked off at the first signs of spring.

Herbs for Cooking

Basil (Annual)

Different varieties include lettuce leaf, sweet and dark opal basil. Grow basil in a sunny area and keep it watered. Pinch as it grows.

Uses: Basil is used in Italian and southern French cooking. It is a basic ingredient in Pesto sauce.

Bay (Perennial)

Bay appears as an evergreen shrub or tree. Plant bay in well drained soil in a sunny, sheltered area away from cold winds.

Uses: Bay is used in "bouquet garni", for soups, sauces, and stews.

Borage (Annual)

Fuzzy leaves and blue flowers distinguish this herb. Plant borage in full sun with good drainage. Pick leaves before they become too hairy.

Uses: Borage leaves have a cucumber flavor and are a nice addition to any vegetable salad.

Chervil (Annual)

Chervil is characterized by lacy green leaves and white flowers. Grow chervil in a warm, lightly shaded area with sufficient moisture.

Uses: Chervil, from the parsley and fennel family, has a slightly sweet flavor which blends well with fish and egg dishes.

169

Chives *(Perennial)*

Chives have grass-like leaves that grow to about 12 inches high. The flowers are a pinky-purple and should be picked to encourage growth. Cut, do not pull chives. They do well in the sun or partial shade.

Uses: Use them as you would onion, garlic or leeks. They do better frozen rather than dried.

Coriander *(Annual)*

The bright green leaves of coriander almost resemble Italian parsley. It is also called cilantro or Mexican parsley. Coriander is grown from seeds sown in spring. Select a light, well-drained area for growing.

Uses: Coriander has a strong, pungent odor and is used in Mexican, Indian, and Chinese cooking. Use the leaves and the seeds that the unpicked flowers form.

Curry Plant *(Perennial)*

This is a small shrub-like plant with sharp grey-green leaves. The curry plant needs full sun and a well-drained soil.

Uses: Add a few sprigs of this plant to rice as it is cooking to give the flavor of curry. Remove sprigs after rice is cooked.

Dill *(Annual)*

This herb is recognized by its feathery leaves, yellow flowers and brown seeds that follow. Dill can grow three feet high. Plant dill in a sunny, well-drained area.

Uses: What would a pickle be without dill? But, dill also can be used in homemade bread, sauces, fresh sausage ,and with fish.

Bergamot *(Perennial)*
Dark green leaves and big red flowers are characteristic of bergamot. Some varieties have flower colors that range from white to deep pink. Bergamot prefers rich, moist soil in a partially shaded area.

Uses: Its leaves have a strong citrus flavor that resembles the Bergamot orange.

Chamomile *(Perennial)*
A low-growing herb with greenish-grey leaves and a flower that resembles a daisy. It prefers the sun and sandy soil.

Uses: Chamomile makes a soothing tea and is good as a rinse for blond hair.

Lemon Verbena *(Perennial)*
It has light green leaves and bears flowers in late summer. Verbena likes light, well-drained soil and a sheltered area.

Uses: Lemon Verbena leaves give a strong citrus flavor to tea. The leaves also make a nice garnish for lemonade and punch.

Mint *(Perennial)*
This herb is one of the easiest to grow. Some of the varieties of mint include spearmint, peppermint, pineapple mint, apple mint, and orange mint. The colors of mint leaves range from grey-green to bright green. Plant mint in moist soil and a slightly shaded area.

Uses: Mint is used not only in beverages or as a garnish, but also to enhance the flavor of lamb and peas. Of course, it is the essence of mint sauce. A sprig of mint added to mint julep is a Southern must!

Clove Pink *(Perennial)*
There are red, pink or white varieties. Pinks like sunny well-drained beds.

Uses: Their carnation, clove-like scent makes them ideal for potpourri and sachets.

Lavender *(Perennial)*
It is a rounded bush with silver grey leaves and pale to deep purple-blue flowers. Lavender needs full sun and a dry soil.

Uses: Lavender can be used in sachet pillows, potpourri, and scented wreaths. Place a sprig or sprigs of lavender in the linen closet for a heavenly scent, or crush several sprigs of lavender under hot running water to scent the bath.

Scented Geranium *(Perennial)*
There are several varieties such as clove, nutmeg, lemon, and rose. Scented geraniums have soft green leaves and small white or pink flowers. They need sun and well-drained soil and do well as house plants.

Uses: Leaves can be used to garnish salads and flavor drinks and cakes. Dried scented geraniums are essential in potpourri.

Lemon Balm *(Perennial)*
Leaves are bright green and have a delightful lemon scent and flavor. This plant prefers some shade but will grow in full sun; balm needs good drainage and moist soil.

Uses: Grind lemon balm in a disposal to give a citrus scent to your kitchen. It can also be used in potpourri.

Herb Recipes

SAUCE VERTE
(for poached fish)

Yield 1 cup

¾ cup homemade mayonnaise
1 T lemon juice

¼ cup finely chopped fresh
    herbs (parsley, chives, dill,
    basil, watercress)

Mix thoroughly and chill

PESTO

Yield 1 cup

2 cups fresh basil
½ cup olive oil
2 garlic cloves
½ cup freshly grated parmesan
    cheese

½ cup pine nuts
1 tsp. salt

Puree the basil, oil, garlic, salt, and pine nuts in blender or food processor. Stir in cheese. Serve at room temperature over hot pasta.

SORREL SOUP

Yield 5 to 6 cups

6 cups chopped sorrel leaves
3 Tbs. Butter

5 cups chicken stock
1 potato cut in small cubes

Sauté sorrel leaves until wilted in butter. Add chicken stock and potato. Cook until potato is tender. Remove from heat and cool. Puree in food processor. Serve hot or cold.

Note: Don't forget herbs when grilling for added aroma and flavor. Sprinkle a bunch of fresh or dried herbs on top of hot coals. Use mint and rosemary for lamb, coriander for chicken, pineapple sage for pork.

Editor's Note:
Come the good ole summer time, mint sherbet served with chocolate brownies is an unsurpassed Southern dessert!

MINT SHERBET

6 Tbs. mint leaves
6 oranges, juiced
2 lemons, juiced
2 cups sugar

2 cups water
½ pint heavy cream
1 stiffly beaten egg white

Set mint leaves aside to soak in juices about 30 minutes. Strain. Cook sugar and water 5 minutes. Add to juices. Chill. Freeze in crank or electric freezer until mushy. Beat egg white until stiff and fold in heavy cream. Add to freezer when juice mixture is mushy. Continue freezing.

Container Gardening

Container gardening has been with us for some time, but it is more popular than it has ever been. Due to its flexibility and mobility, container gardening has allowed the apartment dweller, the busy veteran gardener, the shut-in, and the frequent mover to grow flowers, fruits, vegetables, vines, shrubs, and trees in any container that will hold soil – boxes, bowls, tubs, plastic pots, clay pots, ceramic pots, straw baskets, hanging baskets, and even pillow-pack in plastic bags.

Container gardening allows one to plant where there is no dirt: on a roof top, a penthouse terrace, a balcony, outside staircase, or even a fire escape.

Container plants have different soil, water, fertilizer, and cultural requirements than plants in the ground; however, by supplying a few basic requirements, pleasure and satisfaction will be most rewarding for you to share with your guests. Beauty must be shared to enjoy.

Garden stores and nurseries sell a wide variety of container mixes which are composed of organic materials, sand, and inorganic fillers. The organic part may be various mixtures of peat moss, wood sawdust, or barks. The inorganic fillers may be vermiculite, perlite, or sand. Whatever the mixture, it must provide fast drainage of water, air in the soil after drainage, and a reservoir of water in the soil after drainage.

Most important is the drainage which allows the roots air for growth and respiration. Without sufficient air around the roots, a plant will suffocate. Most pre-mixed potting soils contain few nutrients – add a long lasting slow release fertilizer, about 1/4 cup to 1 gallon of potting soil, and mix well before planting.

One advantage to a ready-mix is its light weight, making the container easier to move about. If necessary, sand and top soil may be added to give stability to top-heavy plants. If one is a "make my own" gardener, the soil mix proportion should be about as follows: 5 parts garden loam soil, 4 parts organic matter, and 1 part coarse builder's sand or an inorganic substitute. Add a few ounces of a complete fertilizer such as 8-8-8, 10-10-10, or equivalent at the rate of one teaspoon per gallon of water. Keep the soil preparation simple, as almost all plants require the same soil mixture. The soil should be a good top soil, preferably taken from a place where plants have grown well, such as a good cultivated

175

garden site, flower bed, or woods. Satisfactory organic matter includes peat moss, leaf mold compost, or well-rotted manure. Inorganic ingredients which aid in providing the proper water-air relationship are vermiculite and perlite. Mix and store in a container, possibly a large garbage can.

Container plants will generally grow well for 3 or more years without repotting if the planting mixture is good. Repot every 3 or 4 years to avoid problems of soil compaction and the reduction of organic matter. Routine fertilizing with a complete fertilizer is necessary for container gardening to compensate for the loss of nutrients from watering.

The frequency of watering will depend upon the soil mix and the weather. During hot sunny days a plant will require more water than on cloudy, cooler days. A plant can become water-logged if it is not drained properly. A porous clay pot will require more frequent watering than a plastic pot. Watering devices such as a watering wand or mist nozzle make the task of watering easier.

If saucers are used, be sure there is pea gravel in the saucer to allow drainage so that the plant does not become waterlogged. Elevating the pot keeps the drainage holes from blocking.

In the selection of containers, keep in mind how much mobility is needed; if mobility is important, select pots or stands on casters. A dolly or handtruck is a handy gadget to have on hand.

Plants in containers are not immune to garden pests – particularly the moisture-seeking pests such as snails and slugs. Place snail bait on a lettuce leaf near the container for several days to lure the slugs and snails away. Then sprinkle the bait around and under pots. The frequent watering required for container plants provides the opportunity to check for pests and, if necessary, to assess what is needed for control.

If one doesn't have a friendly and obliging neighbor, vacation conditioning can be achieved by the use of watering wicks and saucers; however, this method cannot be used for too long a period. A wick can be made of glass wool, fraying the end that goes into the soil, or a nylon clothes line. Special wicks are also available. Place the frayed end in the soil and the other end in a pan of water.

Winterizing is an important part of container gardening. Watch the gardening column in your daily newspaper for weather news to prepare for protection from weather.

The satisfaction and beauty derived from container gardening is never ending. Consider the following:

A lovely lady confined to her wheel chair in a home for the aged repaying your visit with a plant she grew from a leaf in her window-ledge African Violet garden or the enthusiasm and joy of a shut-in watching the tomatoes, growing in tubs, ripen outside her windows.

Giant terracotta dish pots filled with bulbs and pansies on a terrace entrance.

Oaken tubs filled with brilliant red geraniums in a western sun exposure of a country home.

Old sand colored jugs filled with white geraniums on the brick border of a reflecting pool in an enclosed garden.

A vacation retreat with wild flowers and a pot or so of "grocery store" plants on a deck overlooking a lake, giving the "in residence" effect with minimum effort.

A shopping mall atrium with marigolds and ageratum in brilliant array.

Beautiful ferns hanging on chains from grand old oak trees, gently swinging in the breeze.

Terracotta pots of boxwood outlining a terrace walkway to a lower terrace overlooking a bayou, giving a pleasing year-round green.

Straw baskets filled with greenery and blooming violets.

A border of mixed blossoms growing in containers on a terrace of an apartment complex.

A straw basket on a coffee table filled with ivy and one single rose.

Fabulous baskets on stands filled with cascading chrysanthemums in the fall and impatiens in the spring as at Bellingrath Gardens.

Let your imagination go and enjoy container gardening!

Plants Suitable for Containers

A patio with few or no planting areas can be corrected by the use of potted or tub plants, especially in new homes. Due to the size of large tub or pot plants, it is often advisable to choose permanent or winter hardy plants for patio accents rather than those that must be brought indoors for winter protection. Plants often used in the landscape provide a larger size plant for pots and tubs and thus are in better scale to the patio area.

The following are permanent, cold-hardy plants which are very adaptable to pot culture:

Boxwood	Holly Fern	Mahonia
Bamboo	Pittosporum	Yucca
Nandina	Fatshedera	Fatsia
Dwarf Holly	Japanese Maple	Yaupon
Black Pine	Japanese Yew	Dwarf Yaupon
Aucuba Japonica		Crape Myrtle
Loquat (Japanese Plum)		
Aspidistra (Cast Iron Plant)		
Yeddo (Indian Hawthorn)		

Of course, there are also numerous smaller, less permanent plants suitable to hanging baskets and other containers.

Annuals and perennials:

Ageratum	Geranium	Lantana
Begonia	Fig Vine	Ivy
Asian Jasmine	Fern	Hosta
Hibiscus	Pansy	Periwinkle
Impatiens	Portulaca	Viola
Petunia	Sweet Alyssum	Peperomia
Verbena	Shasta Daisy	Snow-in-Summer
Nasturtium	Coleus	Coreopsis
Caladium	Cactus	

Bulbs:

Tulip	Daffodil	Anemone
Canna	Crocus	Amaryllis

Ornamental Grasses:

Liriope	Mondo Grass	Pampas Grass
Monkey Grass		

Herbs

This is only a partial list. Be creative. Try your own favorites.

Gardening With Children

A love of flowers and growing plants is a wonderful legacy to give your children. We all enjoy watching toddlers in the garden noticing bright blossoms at their own eye level (if too many aren't picked!)

When the wild violets in my flower beds bloom, it is a happy memory that the original plants were dug in the woods by teenagers who admired their beauty and planted them for enjoyment. A note of caution about wildflowers: The laws of many states protect certain types of wildflowers and other plants. Scarce specimens that are endangered cannot be picked or dug. Remember this rhyme when collecting from nature:

"If of this plant you don't see many,
Then be a good guy and don't pick any!"

I will never forget the centerpiece for a picnic lunch in the mountains years ago. This unexpected contribution of a nine year old was made from dried sagebrush branches and a handful of wildflowers. Was this inspired by the dining room centerpiece his mother attempted after hearing a Garden Club program on "Driftwood Arrangements"?

Encouraging interest in flowers and plants at an early age often results in adult pleasures and hobbies. The following suggestions might interest young people:

1. Place brightly colored fall leaves between two sheets of waxed paper and press inside a thick book or under a heavy object. This interest could lead to preserving branches of fall foliage. Crush the stems of branches; then place them in tall containers of one part glycerin to three parts warm water. This is absorbed into the leaves and makes them pliable so they don't shed. Small, thin, branches absorb more glycerin water.

   Older children would enjoy preserving blossoms in silica gel. Directions are on the container. Directions for drying flowers in the microwave oven are in the cookbook <u>Tout de Suite à la Microwave II</u> by Jean K. Durkee or are available from your county agent.

2. Airplane plants are easily propagated by pruning baby plants from the large plant when the roots are about 1/2" long. Plant these cuttings in small containers or cups filled with potting soil. Add water and keep moist.

3. Place a sweet potato in a narrow neck vase or glass. A beautiful green vine will grow out of it. Buy the potato from a farmer's market, if possible, to be certain it has not been dried or chemically treated.

   Set the narrow, pointed end of the potato in a jar of water. The roots grow from this end. If you don't have a jar that is the right size, stick toothpicks into the potato to support it at the mouth of the container.

   Place the jar in a warm, dark place. Keep adding water as it is used up. The new roots will grow out first, and in about ten days the stems will start. As soon as the stems appear, move the sweet potato into a sunny or brightly lighted window. Soon the whole potato will become covered with stems and leaves that trail over the sides of the container. (One drop of household bleach added to the water in the jar will eliminate the unpleasant smell that comes from long-standing water.)

4. The carrot root is easy to grow, too. First take off the wilted leaves from the top of the carrot. Then cut off two inches of the carrot at the big end. Set the cut-off piece in a shallow bowl of water with pebbles or stones around it to hold it in place. Change the water often. Keep it one-half inch deep. When roots appear, plant the carrot in a pot filled with moist sand. Keep your new plant well watered, and put it in a sunny window. It will look like a fern. Beets and turnips can be grown the same way.

5. Force paper white narcissus. Line a bowl with about one to two inches of pebbles. Put the bulbs on top of them, flat end (root end) down. The bulbs should be close together but not touching. Add charcoal bits to keep water sweet. Put in more pebbles until only about one-half inch of the bulbs stick up. Pour water in until it touches the bottom of bulbs. Keep the water at this level, but no higher.

   Put the bowl in a cool, dark place for two to three weeks for the bulbs to root. A closet is a good place for this. When the bulbs sprout and growth is two to three inches tall, move to a light (but not direct sunlight), warm location. Flowers should appear in two weeks.

   They can also be planted in soil in an ordinary clay pot, eight to ten inches across the top. Place a piece of gravel over the drainage hole and fill the pot halfway with

180

soil – the richest available, even compost. Place bulbs on top of soil and cover, with just the tips of the bulbs showing. These should be below the top rim of pot.

Put the whole pot in kitchen sink to soak up water from the bottom until the surface of the soil appears damp. Now place in a storage room or dark closet for about two weeks. After the pale green top has grown to about two inches, remove from the closet and bring into light - not hot direct sunlight.

6. Wash eggshells and make a pinhole in the bottom of each one. Place a few pebbles for drainage in them; then fill with potting soil. Plant 2 or 3 seeds in each. Water with a spoon or an eye dropper to keeping from washing the seeds away. Sweet alyssum, herbs, dwarf zinnas or marigolds, even rye grass are good seeds to use. The shells may be dyed if you like. Bright string can be tied around the eggs to make hanging baskets for doll houses.

7. Have you ever thought about making an outside window box from a cardboard milk or juice container (1/2 gallon size)? Your first step is to seal the pouring spout on an empty, rinsed container. Masking or electrical tape is best for sealing. Next, cut out one side of the container, then punch six drainage holes in the bottom of the container with a large nail. Fill the box almost to the top with packaged soil mix. Settle the soil by gently tapping the container on a hard surface, never pushing or packing it. Add enough water to make the soil moist – not wet. Use a pencil or your finger to create a gully or row for the seeds. About four rows will fit the container.

The easiest flowers to grow in this way are annuals, such as zinnias, marigolds, etc. Dwarf varieties would be in scale for this small container.

Plant the seeds about twice as deep as they are wide. Place the seeds in the gullies, cover with soil, and water.Place the container in a waterproof plate to collect excess water and place in a sunny window, indoors. When the soil feels dry, add water, especially in the beginning as the seeds germinate. Once the seedlings have grown three to four inches high, move your window box outdoors after the danger of frost is over.

8. By the time a child is about four years old he might enjoy having a garden of his own. Ensure success by giving the

garden a good start in a sunny location. Turn the soil at least six to eight inches deep, working in a 2 to 3 inch layer of compost.

Buy seeds that are large and quick to germinate. Suitable vegetables include radishes, beans, squash, pumpkins, and cherry tomatoes. When the vegetables are served for dinner, your child will enjoy the produce from his own garden. Include some flowers for color too. Zinnias, nasturtiums, and sunflowers are good choices.

Let your child select a few bedding plants of his own choice at the nursery. These can be planted in a special section of the garden. Guide him in making a selection of hardy plants so he won't be discouraged by failure.

9. Cultivate a child's interest in gardening with children's books on flowers and gardens:

> The Secret Garden by Frances Hodgson Burnett.
>
> Peter Rabbit's Gardening Book, with illustrations by Beatrix Potter.
>
> Plants for Kids to Grow Indoors by Adele Millard.
>
> Play with Plants by Millicent E. Selsam.
>
> The Kid's Garden Book by Patricia Petrich.
>
> Growing Up Green by Alice Skelsey and Gloria Huckaby.

Attracting Wildlife to Our Southern Gardens

Isn't it a shame that we generally feel wildlife attracted to our gardens is lagniappe? With careful planning of our landscape scheme, we can have both– a beautiful garden and an abundance of native fauna. Common sense, gained by observation in your local area and augmented by a few good books, will provide you with the correct formula.

First, consider the three factors that attract wildlife – water, cover, and food. Offer these in proper balance and your garden becomes a mecca for birds and animals.

Next, consider your special requirements: is it a small city lot bare of plants, an old, established city home, a farm, or a suburban home? All of these have special merits and limitations to be considered.

Last, but not least, study the type of wildlife you wish to attract. Birds are the most common and safest creatures, but they come in two classes: some perch to eat while others love to scratch. The latter will sometimes cause damage to small plants if the food source is too close. Squirrels, raccoons, and opossums are cute "critters" to observe and are relatively common even in large cities. To lessen their impact in cities, provision should be made for nesting boxes, so that they will be less likely to invade your home looking for shelter. Of course, plenty of their favorite food should be provided. Opossums make excellent garbage disposals. Deer are in a class of their own and are usually unwanted after their first visit! They are no longer a rare sight in the country gardens and occasionally are sighted in suburban areas.

If you have the option of building a new home on a wooded lot, you are indeed lucky. This gives you the opportunity to protect a few native trees and shrubs from the builder, putting you years ahead in landscaping, for most trees require ten to thirty years to reach fruit-bearing age. Oaks, red mulberries, hackberries, and sweetgums are all large deciduous trees that should be considered. Red cedar and American holly are excellent large evergreen trees often found growing on existing wooded acreage. Do not make the beginner's mistake and leave too many large trees, for the understory shrubs need sunlight, too.

The "bread and butter" plants for wildlife are usually fruiting shrubs from two to twenty feet in height. Most species grow rapidly and can be added to old or new landscapes. If your budget permits, fruiting-size shrubs can be purchased, or with care and root pruning before digging, moved from the wild without ill effect. This should only be done if the plant is abundant in the wild or if it is in danger of being destroyed.

A common sense method of selecting native shrubs for your area is to observe plants growing in an old fence row. These were seeded by resting birds and are a witness to the birds' preference in your locality. In our area, Indian cherry *(Rhamnus caroliniana)*, yaupon *(Ilex vomitoria)*, wax myrtle, *(Myrica cerifera)*, and sumac *(Rhus copallina)* are most common. We recommend wax myrtle and yaupon for screening and cover as well as for being excellent fruiting plants. However, you must remember that they are dioecious, so be sure to plant a female to get one that bears fruit. The red buckeye *(Aesclus pavia)* is a must for the ruby-throated hummingbird. We have noticed that they time their arrival to coincide with the blossoming of the red buckeye. If you worry about the poisonous "buckeye" seed, simply remove the flower-head when it has finished blooming.

A number of perennials and annuals attract birds. Thistles, sunflowers, and grasses that are allowed to mature and go to seed are sought by many bird species. Sometimes the mature grasses are considered unsightly, but use them as specimen plantings in controlled situations, and they will brighten your winter landscape with texture and color.

We have watched the ruby-throated hummingbird make many trips to collect mouthfuls of the soft fluff attached to the seeds of the false dandelion *(Pyrrhopappus carolinianus)*. Nesting material? So what if we do have to spend some time pulling out the extra ones – the flowers are lovely and the exercise is good for us.

Water is a very important part of your landscape. All animals, even the box turtle (terrapin to us), will come to take a drink when it is extremely dry. Water in the right place is as important as any factor in attracting birds. A deep fountain in the center of your bare lawn might appeal to you, but not to a smart bird. The bird knows that if it doesn't drown, the cat or hawk is sure to catch it before it can reach the shelter of a limb to dry its soggy feathers. Place a shallow container of water near or under a shrub with easily accessible limbs for the birds to use in case of danger. If it's too deep, fill with stones to leave a water depth of one-half to one

inch. If the water flows, so much the better. Clean and disinfect regularly to prevent the spread of disease. Remember, providing water year round is a must for the well being of our wildlife.

Most naturalists in my association have their pet list of trees and shrubs for wildlife, and we here at Briarwood are no exception. The following are our selections in order of size, plus the species attracted to them:

Large Trees

Oaks *Quercus,* all species*:*
Squirrels, deer, raccoons, and numerous birds.

Sweetgum *Liquidambar styraciflua:*
The seeds are relished by the goldfinches and pine siskins. Clinging to the sweetgum balls, they pick the seeds out; then those seeds that fall to the ground are eaten by the sparrows and other scratching birds.

Sycamore *Platanus occidentalis:*
A tree that is not recommended for a small garden because of the mess it creates; however, the seeds are eaten by the goldfinches and pine siskins. The white bark is very attractive in winter.

Hackberry *Celtix laevigata*:
Berries for the birds.

Blackgum *Nyssa sylvatica:*
Birds, squirrels, and other animals relish the fruit of this tree. A bonus for us is the beautiful fall color.

Magnolia *Magnolia grandiflora:*
Provides food and shelter for birds and squirrels. Best grown with the limbs coming all the way to the ground to hide some of the leaves it is forever casting off.

Red Cedar *Juniperus virginiana:*
A beautiful evergreen that gives food and shelter but is host to the cedar-apple rust that attacks crabapples.

American Holly *Ilex opaca:*
Squirrels and birds quickly consume the berries!

Hickory *Carya* species:
The nuts are much sought after by the squirrels, plus it usually provides us with fall color.

Pecan *Carya illinoensis:*
As we all know, squirrels, raccoons, crows, and bluejays love the nuts of this tree.

American Beech *Fagus grandifolia:*
Numerous species of birds and animals eat the tasty beech nut. Fortunate is the person who has the right conditions to grow this tree, for it brightens a dreary winter with its leaves turning a lovely tan and hanging on until spring.

Red Mulberry *Morus rubra:*
The fruit is a favorite of squirrels, opossums, raccoons, and most of the birds, especially woodpeckers, thrushes, tanagers. Deer and rabbits, even the box turtle, pick up the ones that happen to fall on the ground.

Pines *Pinus,* all species:
The seeds are eaten by many species of birds and squirrels. Pines also provide screening and cover.

Small Trees and Shrubs

Service Berry *Amelanchier laevis:*
You hardly get a chance to see the small apple-shaped fruit before it is snapped up by the birds. An early-blooming small tree with fall color.

Wild Plums *Prunus,* all species:
Birds and animals love the fruit.

Devilwood *Osmanthus americanus:*
The fruit is quickly consumed by birds and squirrels. Our native sweet olive, it is a good tree to use for screening and cover since it is evergreen. Very fragrant flowers.

Dogwood *Cornus florida:*
Everyone is aware of the dogwood because of its spring bloom, but we are surprised at the number of people who do not know that it produces fruit, a red drupe that is eagerly sought by most birds and animals.

Fringe Tree *Chionanthus virginica:*
Known as grancy grey beard because of its flowers. It blooms as the dogwood is finishing. Do plant a female with the more showy male so the birds and animals can enjoy the fruit.

Crabapple *Malus angustifolia:*
Squirrels, raccoons, and especially deer, love the fruit.

Rusty Black Haw *Viburnum rufidulum:*
A very desirable small tree; the fruit is eaten by birds and animals. We recommend all species of viburnums.

Dahoon Holly *Ilex cassine:*
A small evergreen holly without stickers on the leaves. The fruit is eaten by birds and probably squirrels.

Deciduous Hollies *Ilex decidua and I. verticilata:*
More shrubs than trees, the fruit of these are saved till last by the birds.

Red Buckeye *Aesclus pavia:*
The ruby-throated hummingbird, and sometimes the orchard oriole, come to the flowers.

Fall Elaeagnus *Eleagnus umbellata:*
This exotic is almost as useful as the gum cherry. The fruit ripens in the fall and is eaten by the squirrels, birds, and deer, reaching as high as they can.

Bradford Pear *Pyrus calleryana:*
An introduced species that has small fruit eaten by birds and animals. Wonderful spring bloom and fall color.

Vines

A word of caution – some can quickly become a nusiance. Their abundance attests to how popular they make themselves to birds and animals so that their survival is assured.

Woodbine *Lonicera sempervirens:*
One of the few vines that has no bad habits and is a must for the hummingbirds.

Passion Flower *Passiflora incarnata:*
The fruit, known as maypop, is relished by the raccoons and opossums.

Grapes *Vitis,* all species including the muscadine:
The fruit is an excellent food source for birds and animals; only the muscadine becomes invasive.

Virginia Creeper *Parthenocissus quinquefolia:*
A favorite with the birds. (Poison ivy which is similar has fruit that is a source of food for the birds, too).

Bittersweet *Celastrus scandens:*
Another favorite fruit of the birds.

Ratten *Berchemia scandens:*
The fruit is eaten by the birds and squirrels. It is a deadly constrictor of trees so is not recommended.

Smilax Briars *Smilax* all species:
Two species of smilax are not too obnoxious - *S. walteri* with its red berries and *S. lanceolata*, a beautiful evergreen that adds color in winter. These vines attract birds and squirrels.

BOOKS

Books we have found helpful in learning to attract wildlife to one's gardens:

Plants for the South, Neil G. Odenwald and James R. Turner, Claitor's Publishing Division.

Natives Preferred, Caroline Dorman. Claitor's Publishing Division.

How to Grow Wildflowers and Wild Shrubs and Trees in Your Own Garden, Hal Bruce. Alfred A. Knopf.

The Wild Garden, Violet Stevenson. Penguin Handbooks.

Landscaping with Wildflowers and Native Plants, William H. W. Wison. Ortho Books.

Beyond the Bird Feeder, John V. Dennis. Alfred A. Knopf.

Richard L. Johnson, Curator
Caroline Dorman Nature Preserve - Briarwood
Rt. 1, Box 195
Saline, LA 71070

Conservation is nothing else but good steward-
ship. Since the beginning of man on earth, we have been
cautioned, in essence . . . take care of what you have on
earth, for when it is gone, nothing can recall it. Checks
and balances were placed on everything. It is only when
we, in our ignorance or greed, upset the balance that
things get out of control. If each person, no matter
where he lives, would practice conservation, there
would be no problem with pollution of land and water
and air. We are just a link in the chain of living things.
Each time we destroy a plant or animal into extinction,
the chain is weakened, until someday in the future man
may be the only link left – and there is no way we could
survive! The outcome depends on us.

Richard L. Johnson

Garden Terms

Accent plant - single plant or small groups of plants for emphasis in the garden.

Acidify - to change pH of the soil to acid. Use aluminum sulfate (cautiously) to cause a "sour" soil. Camellias and azaleas need acid soil.

Aeration - air circulation in soil to keep from packing or becoming water logged. Sand, peat, leafmold help aerate soil.

Aphids - plant lice attacking every garden or houseplant. Use contact insecticides to control.

Bone meal - fertilizer made from ground up animal bones, and so on. Slow acting, non-burning.

Botanical name - Latin name used for international communication usually consisting of 2 or 3 words. The genus (a group marked by common characteristics or by one characteristic) is first; second is the specific epithet (e.g. Vinca rosea). A 3rd or even 4th word may be added to designate a subdivision.

Biennial - plant started from seed requiring two growing seasons to grow and bloom (e.g. hollyhock).

Budding - method of propagation; form of grafting in which a single bud or a desired variety with little or no wood is inserted in the understock.

Chlorophyll - the green substance of leaves and plants necessary for the process of photosynthesis.

Cold frame - bottomless box placed on the soil or a pit in which plants may be started, grown, or stored.

Conifer - woody plant with seeds in cones; it does not have fruit or flowers.

Cultivar - a plant resulting from selective hybridization.

Damping off - when plants rot at the roots due to fungus disease often encouraged by poor drainage or over watering.

Deciduous - a tree or bush which sheds it leaves annually.

Dioecious - a group of plants having separate sexes. Only the female bears fruit.

Drupe - a fleshy fruit containing usually one hard-coated seed.

Dormancy - a period of rest; an inactive state due to unfavorable environmental conditions or as an internal physiological control.

Espalier - to train a plant in a fixed pattern, usually flat against a wall or fence.

Evergreen - a plant that retains foliage from season to season; can be either broadleaf or conifer (e.g. live oak, pine).

Eye - usually an underveloped bud on a tuber which will sprout after the tuber is planted.

Fungicide - material used to protect plants or kill fungus usually by spraying. There are two varieties: eradicants kill fungi; protectants prevent fungi.

Fungus - member of a low order of plants which subsist on live or dead organic matter. Reproduces by spores.

Habitat - region where a plant grows naturally or is indigenous.

Hardening - conditioning cut flowers for longer life. Refer to the charts in "Care of Cut Material."

Hardening off - practice of toughening young plants started indoors or under glass to accustom them to outdoors.

Heeling in - temporary storage of a plant by covering with soil or leaves.

Herbaceous border - a border in which herbaceous plants (those which die to the ground) are used rather than shrubs or evergreens.

Herbicide - a substance used for killing plants, especially weeds.

Hot bed - a bottomless box with transparent, removable top used to grow plants out of season, differing from a cold frame in that it is artificially heated.

Hot house (greenhouse) - a glass or plastic covered house for growing plants kept artificially heated or heated by the sun.

Humus - thoroughly decomposed organic or non-mineral material that makes up a large part of good, fertile, productive soil (e.g. leaves, pine straw, wood chips, citrus fruit peels, etc.).

Hybrid - plant of mixed origin; a result of cross fertilization.

Inflorescence - the flowering part of the plant.

Insecticide - a chemical product of natural or synthetic origin used to kill insects that infest plants.

Leader - upright tip of any tree or shrub which grows with the center trunk; the main trunk.

Leaf mold - a natural humus made from rotting leaves, grass clippings, etc.

Monoecious - male and female flowers on the same plant.

Panicle - any loose, diversely branching flower cluster.

Peat moss - humus material derived from sphagnum moss or other plants used to loosen soil; also used as mulch to keep down grass and retain moisture around plants.

Perlite - a course, light-weight volcanic glass used to loosen soil, especially potting soil.

Pesticide - method of killing garden enemies, usually by spraying or sprinkling on the ground.

pH - potential hydrogen ("H" being the symbol of Hydrogen). The degree of acidity or alkalinity. Seven (7) is neutral, above 7 is alkaline, and below 7 is acid. "Sweet" soil is alkaline.

Runner (stolon) - a long, slender, trailing branch which may take root and produce new plants wherever leaf or bud parts come in contact with soil. (e.g. strawberry, ajuga).

Spore - a simple, detached cell for asexual reproduction (e.g. ferns, fungi).

Sprigging - planting small divisions of plants, as in border grass.

Subcanopy - See woody plants.

Sucker - a shoot which springs from a bud at the summit of the roots, especially in grafted plants.

191

Systemic - a toxic ingredient absorbed by a plant so as to be lethal to sucking insects that feed on it.

Tap root - the central root descending downward with side roots from it.

Thinning - pulling up plants that have come up too thick so that plants left may grow stronger.

Topiary - training or pruning plant material into unnatural geometric or fantastic shapes.

Top soil - soil taken from top inches of ground where most plants get their nutrients and water.

Understock (stock) - plant on which a cutting may be propagated (e.g. sasanqua on which to graft camellia).

Understory - small trees or shrubs growing under a large tree (e.g. understory tree - dogwood).

Vascular plant - plant with vessels or ducts in its stems to conduct fluids.

Vermiculite - a mica mineral used to aerate potting soil. It helps hold moisture and nutrients but is fragile and eventually breaks down.

Woody plants - usually divided into 4 groups:

> **canopy** - large trees forming a canopy over plant material (e.g. oak, pine).
>
> **subcanopy** - smaller trees under the large trees (e.g. red bud, dogwood).
>
> **shrub** - plants under small trees (e.g. azaleas).
>
> **subshrub** - smallest woody plants (e.g. creeping juniper, dwarf gardenia).
>
> (These are most often ecological terms.)

Index

193

196

GARDENING FOR SOUTHERN SEASONS
Monroe Garden Study League
P.O. Box 2152
Monroe, LA 71207

Please send me _____ copies @ $14.95 each $ _____

Add postage and handling @ $2.00 each $ _____

Louisiana residents add 8½% sales tax @ $1.30 each $ _____

TOTAL ENCLOSED $ _____

Name _____

Address _____

City _____ State _____ Zip _____

Please make checks payable to Monroe Garden Study League

GARDENING FOR SOUTHERN SEASONS
Monroe Garden Study League
P.O. Box 2152
Monroe, LA 71207

Please send me _____ copies @ $14.95 each $ _____

Add postage and handling @ $2.00 each $ _____

Louisiana residents add 8½% sales tax @ $1.30 each $ _____

TOTAL ENCLOSED $ _____

Name _____

Address _____

City _____ State _____ Zip _____

Please make checks payable to Monroe Garden Study League